I0748874

Gratitude EXPRESSIONS

ꝏ

A Collection of Treasures

Gratitude Expressions
ISBN 978-0-9823220-1-7

Published by Gratitude Partners, LLC
2655 Curryville Road
Chuluota, Florida 32766
Phone (407) 977-8080
Fax (407) 977-8078
For more information or to order a copy of this book,
visit *GratitudeExpressions.com* or call 407.977.8080
Printed in the United States of America.

Book Design by Julie Hoyt Dorman

Suggested uses for Gratitude Expressions

For Reliving the Memory— Now and in the Future

Gratitude Expressions is a five-year journal that can help you memorialize and remember your most joyous moments. Consider writing each day about something for which you are thankful. It's fun and uplifting to look back and see how much we have to be grateful for. Here are some ideas:

— Write of what happened to you that caused you to smile — or laugh.

— Write about a pet who always has a happy smile for you.

— Write of someone you recognize as having added value to your life.

— Write a note of thanks about a kindness bestowed upon you.

— Write of what you did that caused someone to smile.

— Write about a stranger who reached out to you.

— Write of a long-forgotten memory that still warms your heart.

— Write of someone who said thanks to you and how that made you feel.

— Write of something in your life that you never want to change and why.

— Write a note of thanks about something — anything.

— Write about a "thank you" you gave someone and how that made you feel.

— Write about a hug you shared with someone.

— Write about a child you saw laughing and how that made you feel.

— Write about a stranger you reached out to.

— Write about a new friend.

TO SPEAK GRATITUDE
IS COURTEOUS AND PLEASANT,
TO ENACT GRATITUDE
IS GENEROUS AND NOBLE,
BUT TO LIVE GRATITUDE IS TO
TOUCH HEAVEN.

—JOHANNES A. GAERTNER

January 1

Year 1

Year 2

Year 3

Year 4

Year 5

January 2

SAYING THANK YOU
IS MORE THAN GOOD MANNERS.
IT IS GOOD SPIRITUALITY.

—ALFRED PAINTER.

Year 1

Year 2

Year 3

Year 4

Year 5

January 3

HAPPINESS CANNOT BE TRAVELED TO, OWNED, EARNED, WORN OR CONSUMED. HAPPINESS IS THE SPIRITUAL EXPERIENCE OF LIVING EVERY MINUTE WITH LOVE, GRACE AND GRATITUDE.

—DENIS WAITLEY

Year 1

Year 2

Year 3

Year 4

Year 5

January 4

GRATITUDE IS THE FAIREST BLOSSOM WHICH SPRINGS FROM THE SOUL.

—HENRY WARD BEECHER.

Year 1

Year 2

Year 3

Year 4

Year 5

GIVE THANKS FOR A LITTLE AND YOU WILL FIND A LOT.

—THE HAUSA OF NIGERIA

January 5

Year 1

Year 2

Year 3

Year 4

Year 5

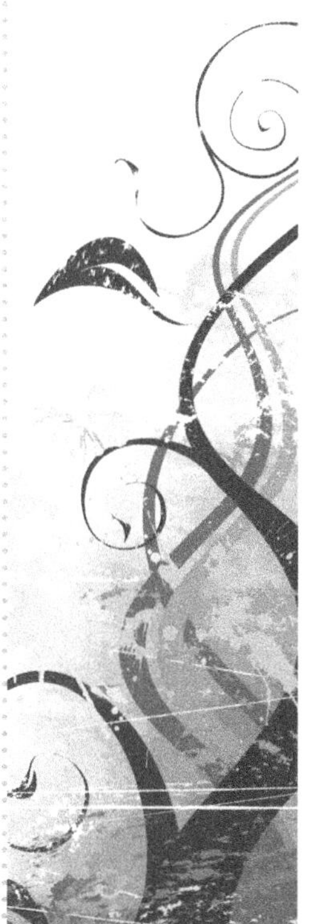

January 6

THE PILGRIMS MADE SEVEN TIMES MORE GRAVES THAN HUTS. NO AMERICANS HAVE BEEN MORE IMPOVERISHED THAN THESE WHO, NEVERTHELESS, SET ASIDE A DAY OF THANKSGIVING.

—H. U. WESTERMAYER

Year 1

Year 2

Year 3

Year 4

Year 5

January 7

THE HARDEST ARITHMETIC
TO MASTER IS THAT WHICH
ENABLES US TO
COUNT OUR BLESSINGS.

—Eric Hoffer

Year 1

Year 2

Year 3

Year 4

Year 5

January 8

TOO OFTEN WE UNDERESTIMATE THE POWER
OF A TOUCH, A SMILE, A KIND WORD,
A LISTENING EAR, AN HONEST COMPLIMENT,
OR THE SMALLEST ACT OF CARING,
ALL OF WHICH HAVE THE POTENTIAL
TO TURN A LIFE AROUND.

—Leo Buscaglia

Year 1

Year 2

Year 3

Year 4

Year 5

January 9

THE WAY TO GAIN A GOOD REPUTATION
IS TO ENDEAVOR TO BE WHAT
YOU DESIRE TO APPEAR.

—SOCRATES

Year 1

Year 2

Year 3

Year 4

Year 5

January 10

WE CAN ONLY BE SAID TO BE ALIVE IN THOSE MOMENTS WHEN OUR HEARTS ARE CONSCIOUS OF OUR TREASURES.

—THORNTON WILDER

Year 1

Year 2

Year 3

Year 4

Year 5

Men are disturbed not by things,
but by the view
which they take of them.

—Epictetus

January 11

Year 1

Year 2

Year 3

Year 4

Year 5

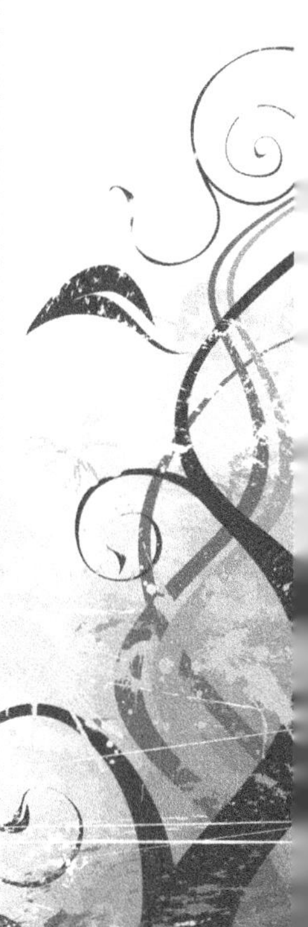

January 12

GRATITUDE IS NOT ONLY
THE GREATEST OF VIRTUES,
BUT THE PARENT OF ALL OTHERS.

—CICERO

Year 1

Year 2

Year 3

Year 4

Year 5

January 13

As we express our gratitude,
we must never forget
that the highest appreciation
is not to utter words,
but to live by them.

—John F. Kennedy

Year 1

Year 2

Year 3

Year 4

Year 5

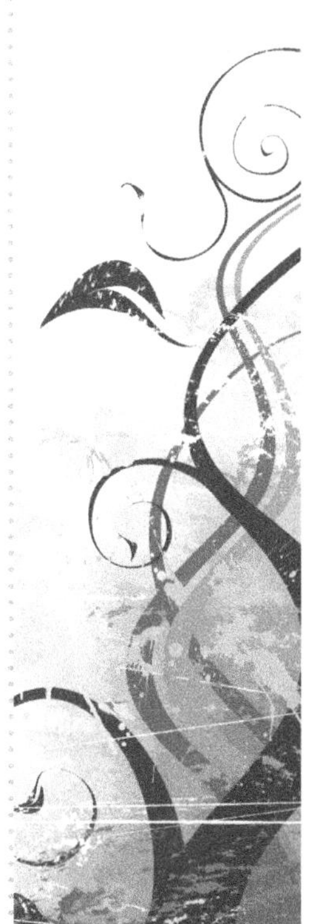

January 14

THE LAW OF GRATITUDE
IS THE NATURAL PRINCIPLE
THAT ACTION AND REACTION
ARE ALWAYS EQUAL,
AND IN OPPOSITE DIRECTIONS.

—Wallace Wattles

Year 1

Year 2

Year 3

Year 4

Year 5

January 15

PRIDE SLAYS THANKSGIVING, BUT A HUMBLE MIND IS THE SOIL OUT OF WHICH THANKS NATURALLY GROWS. A PROUD MAN IS SELDOM A GRATEFUL MAN, FOR HE NEVER THINKS HE GETS AS MUCH AS HE DESERVES.

—HENRY WARD BEECHER

Year 1

Year 2

Year 3

Year 4

Year 5

January 16

ALWAYS REMEMBER,
EVERYONE IS HUNGRY FOR PRAISE
AND STARVING FOR
HONEST APPRECIATION!

—DAVID BRANDT BERG

Year 1

Year 2

Year 3

Year 4

Year 5

THE MORE YOU RECOGNIZE AND
EXPRESS GRATITUDE
FOR THE THINGS YOU HAVE,
THE MORE YOU WILL HAVE
TO EXPRESS GRATITUDE FOR.

—Zig Ziglar

January 17

Year 1

Year 2

Year 3

Year 4

Year 5

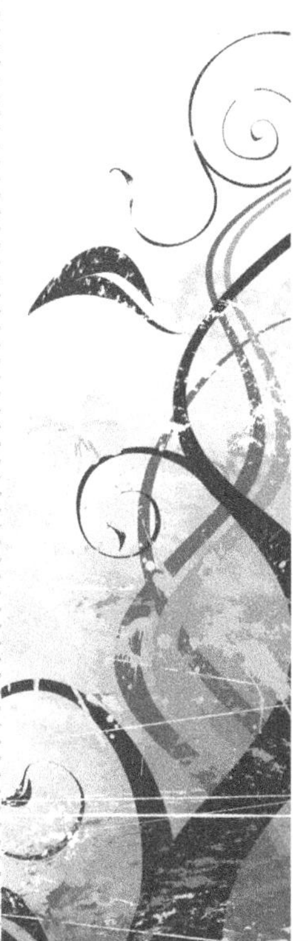

January 18

I awoke this morning with devout thanksgiving for my friends, the old and new. Shall I not call God the Beautiful, who daily showeth Himself so to me in his gifts?

—Ralph Waldo Emerson

Year 1

Year 2

Year 3

Year 4

Year 5

Kind words can be short
and easy to speak,
but their echoes are truly endless.

—Mother Teresa

January 19

Year 1

Year 2

Year 3

Year 4

Year 5

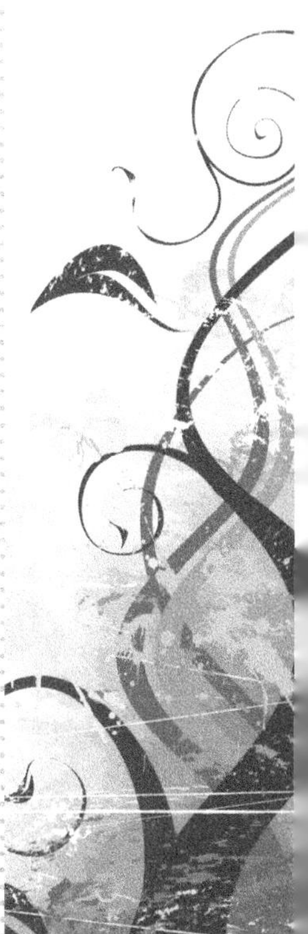

January 20

DON'T PRAY WHEN IT RAINS
IF YOU DON'T PRAY
WHEN THE SUN SHINES.

—LEROY SATCHEL PAIGE

Year 1

Year 2

Year 3

Year 4

Year 5

January 21

YOU CANNOT DO A KINDNESS TOO SOON
BECAUSE YOU NEVER KNOW
HOW SOON IT WILL BE TOO LATE.

—RALPH WALDO EMERSON

Year 1

Year 2

Year 3

Year 4

Year 5

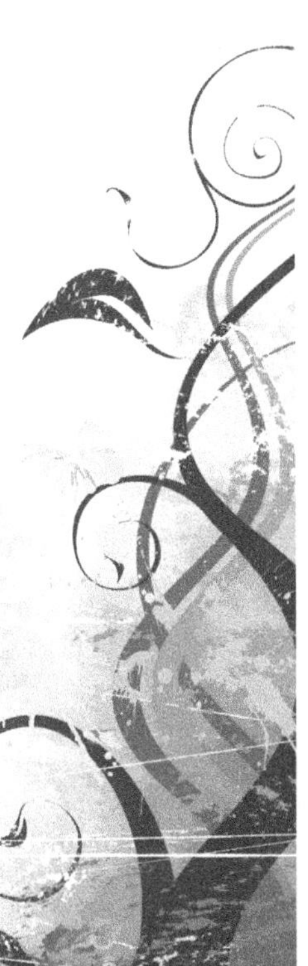

January 22

I THANK YOU GOD FOR THIS
MOST AMAZING DAY, FOR THE LEAPING
GREENLY SPIRITS OF TREES,
AND FOR THE BLUE DREAM OF SKY AND
FOR EVERYTHING WHICH IS NATURAL,
WHICH IS INFINITE, WHICH IS YES.

—E. E. CUMMINGS

Year 1

Year 2

Year 3

Year 4

Year 5

January 23

IF IT IS A NEW THOUGHT TO YOU THAT GRATITUDE BRINGS YOUR WHOLE MIND INTO CLOSER HARMONY WITH THE CREATIVE ENERGIES OF THE UNIVERSE, CONSIDER IT WELL, AND YOU WILL SEE THAT IT IS TRUE.

—WALLACE WATTLES

Year 1

Year 2

Year 3

Year 4

Year 5

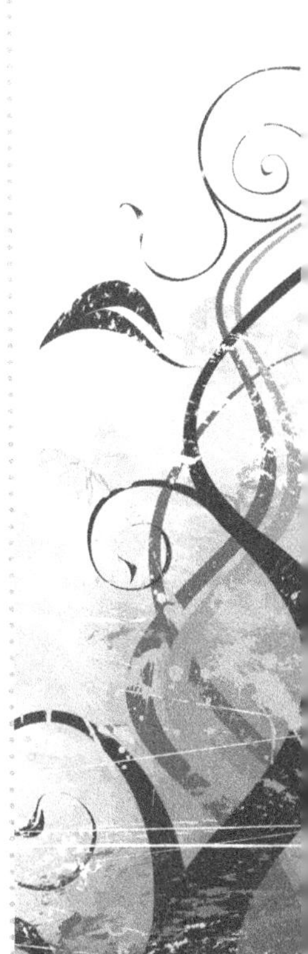

January 24

EVERYONE WANTS TO BE APPRECIATED,
SO IF YOU APPRECIATE SOMEONE,
DON'T KEEP IT A SECRET.

—MARY KAY ASH

Year 1

Year 2

Year 3

Year 4

Year 5

January 25

FLATTERY IS FROM THE TEETH OUT.
SINCERE APPRECIATION IS
FROM THE HEART OUT.

—DALE CARNEGIE

Year 1

Year 2

Year 3

Year 4

Year 5

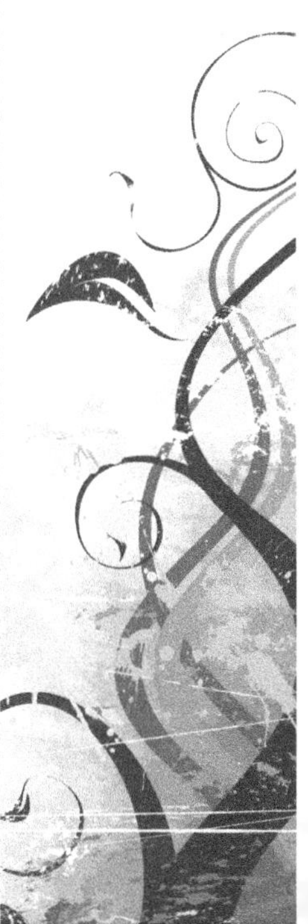

January 26

VIRTUE IS NOT HEREDITARY.

—THOMAS PAINE

Year 1

Year 2

Year 3

Year 4

Year 5

January 27

IN EVERY PERSON
WHO COMES NEAR YOU
LOOK FOR WHAT IS GOOD
AND STRONG.

—JOHN RUSKIN

Year 1

Year 2

Year 3

Year 4

Year 5

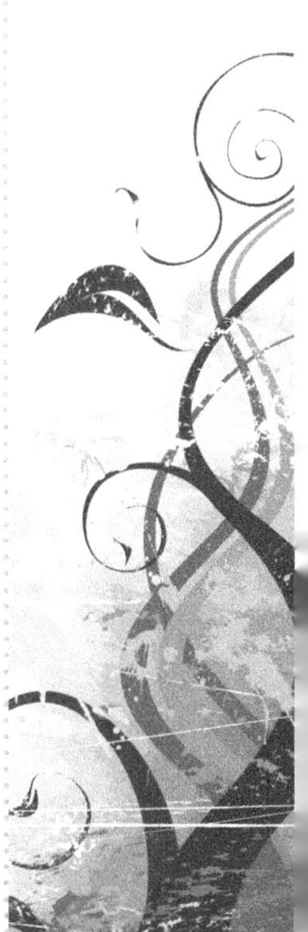

January 28

LET US BE GRATEFUL TO PEOPLE
WHO MAKE US HAPPY;
THEY ARE THE CHARMING GARDENERS
WHO MAKE OUR SOULS BLOSSOM.

—MARCEL PROUST

Year 1

Year 2

Year 3

Year 4

Year 5

A PERSON HOWEVER LEARNED
AND QUALIFIED IN HIS LIFE'S WORK
IN WHOM GRATITUDE IS ABSENT,
IS DEVOID OF THAT BEAUTY OF CHARACTER
WHICH MAKES PERSONALITY FRAGRANT.

—Hazrat Inayat Khan

January 29

Year 1

Year 2

Year 3

Year 4

Year 5

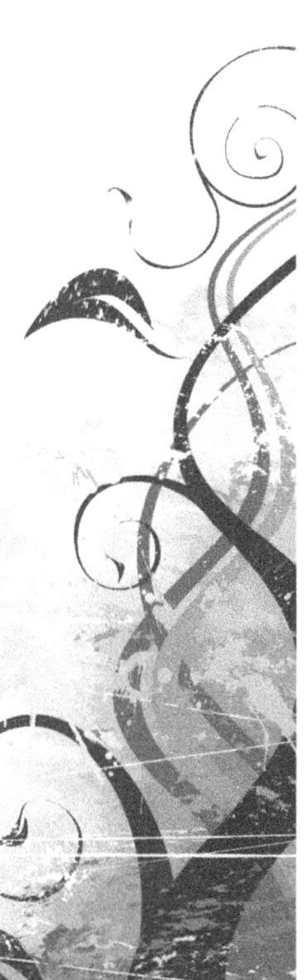

January 30

GRATITUDE IS A DUTY
WHICH OUGHT TO BE PAID,
BUT WHICH NONE
HAVE A RIGHT TO EXPECT.

—JEAN-JACQUES ROUSSEAU

Year 1

Year 2

Year 3

Year 4

Year 5

January 31

APPRECIATION CAN MAKE A DAY,
EVEN CHANGE A LIFE.
YOUR WILLINGNESS TO PUT IT INTO
WORDS IS ALL THAT IS NECESSARY.

—MARGARET COUSINS

Year 1

Year 2

Year 3

Year 4

Year 5

February 1

GIVEN THE AMOUNT OF UNJUST SUFFERING
AND UNHAPPINESS IN THE WORLD,
I AM DEEPLY GRATEFUL FOR, SOMETIMES
EVEN PERPLEXED BY, HOW MUCH MISERY
I HAVE BEEN SPARED.

—DENNIS PRAGER

Year 1

Year 2

Year 3

Year 4

Year 5

February 2

In the New Testament,
religion is grace
and ethics is gratitude.

—Thomas Erskine

Year 1

Year 2

Year 3

Year 4

Year 5

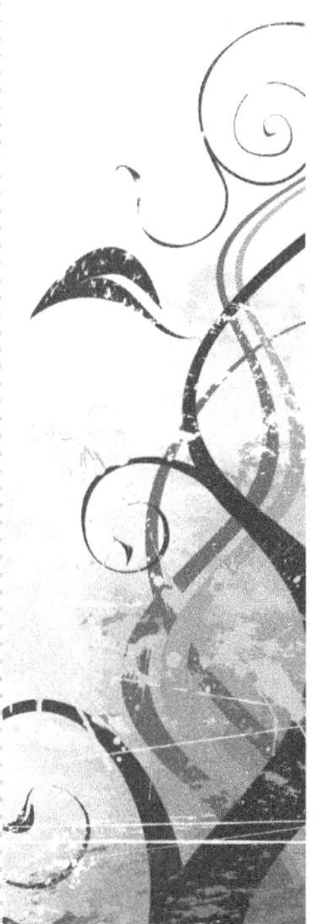

February 3

LET'S CHOOSE TODAY TO QUENCH OUR THIRST FOR THE "GOOD LIFE" WE THINK OTHERS LEAD BY ACKNOWLEDGING THE GOOD THAT ALREADY EXISTS IN OUR LIVES. WE CAN THEN OFFER THE UNIVERSE THE GIFT OF OUR GRATEFUL HEARTS.

—SARAH BAN BREATHNACH

Year 1

Year 2

Year 3

Year 4

Year 5

I had the blues
because I had no shoes
until upon the street,
I met a man who had no feet.

—Denis Waitely

February 4

Year 1

Year 2

Year 3

Year 4

Year 5

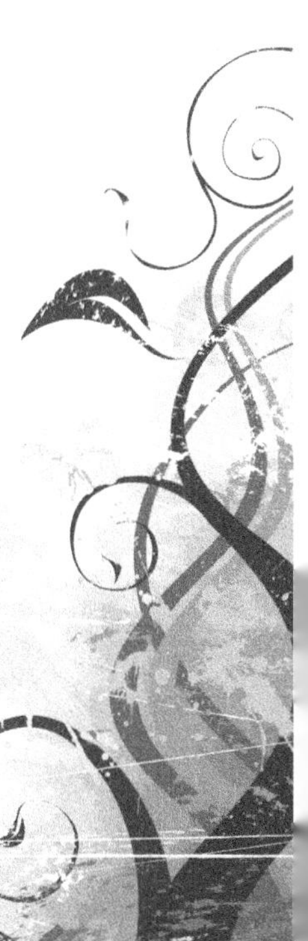

February 5

COUNT YOUR BLESSINGS. ONCE YOU REALIZE HOW VALUABLE YOU ARE AND HOW MUCH YOU HAVE GOING FOR YOU, THE SMILES WILL RETURN, THE SUN WILL BREAK OUT, THE MUSIC WILL PLAY, AND YOU WILL

Year 1

Year 2

Year 3

Year 4

Year 5

FINALLY BE ABLE TO MOVE FORWARD
THE LIFE THAT GOD INTENDED FOR YOU
WITH GRACE, STRENGTH, COURAGE,
AND CONFIDENCE.

—Og Mandino

February 6

Year 1

Year 2

Year 3

Year 4

Year 5

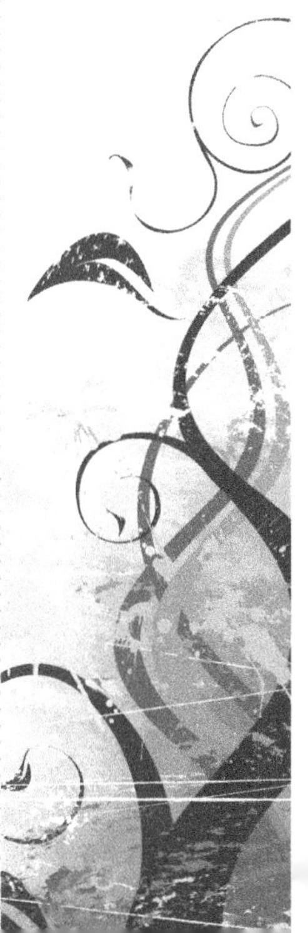

February 7

We are still masters
of our fate.
We are still captains
of our souls.

—Winston Churchill

Year 1

Year 2

Year 3

Year 4

Year 5

February 8

THE PAST CANNOT BE CHANGED;
THE FUTURE IS STILL IN YOUR POWER.

—HUGH WHITE

Year 1

Year 2

Year 3

Year 4

Year 5

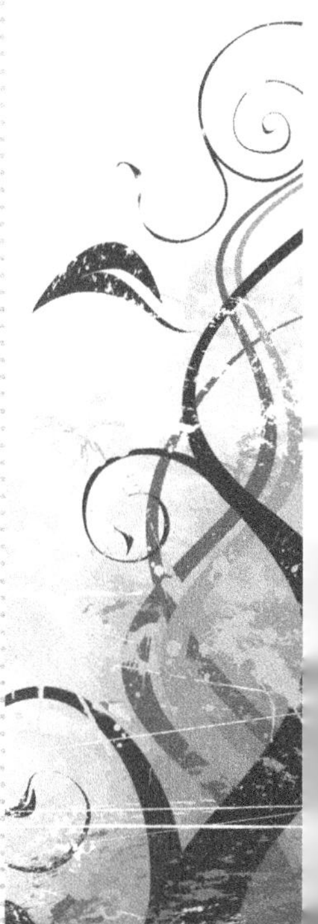

February 9

Remember God's bounty in the year.
String the pearls of His favor.
Hide the dark parts, except so far
as they are breaking out in light!
Give this one day to thanks,
to joy, to gratitude!

—Henry Ward Beecher

Year 1

Year 2

Year 3

Year 4

Year 5

February 10

TAKE FULL ACCOUNT OF WHAT EXCELLENCIES WHICH YOU POSSESS, AND IN GRATITUDE REMEMBER HOW YOU WOULD HANKER AFTER THEM, IF YOU HAD THEM NOT.

—Marcus Aurelius

Year 1

Year 2

Year 3

Year 4

Year 5

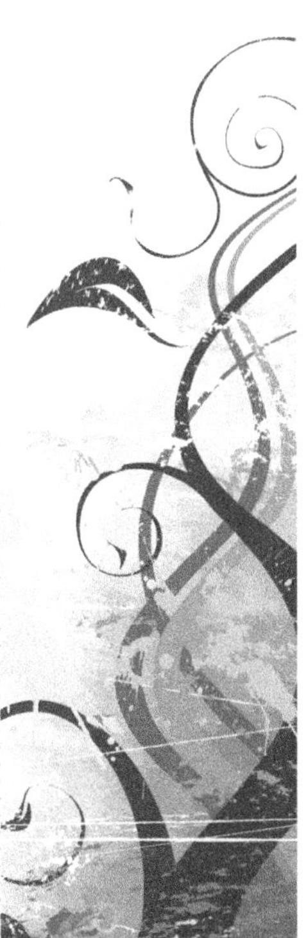

February 11

HAPPINESS DOES NOT CONSIST IN PASTIMES AND AMUSEMENTS BUT IN VIRTUOUS ACTIVITIES.

—ARISTOTLE

Year 1

Year 2

Year 3

Year 4

Year 5

NO ONE WHO ACHIEVES SUCCESS DOES SO WITHOUT ACKNOWLEDGING THE HELP OF OTHERS. THE WISE AND CONFIDENT ACKNOWLEDGE THIS HELP WITH GRATITUDE.

—AUTHOR UNKNOWN

February 12

Year 1

Year 2

Year 3

Year 4

Year 5

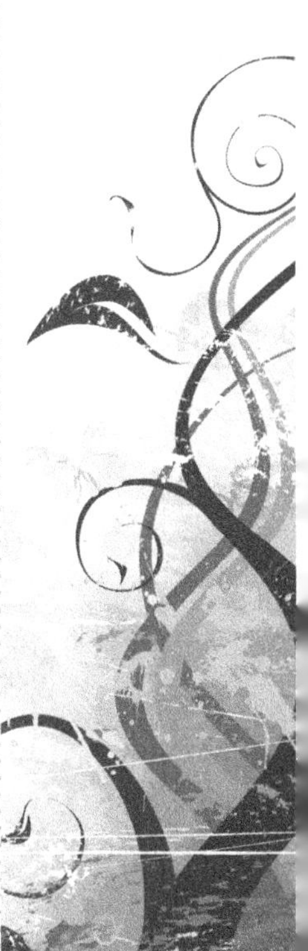

February 13

YOU SHALL REJOICE IN ALL THE GOOD THINGS THE LORD YOUR GOD HAS GIVEN TO YOU AND YOUR HOUSEHOLD.

—DEUTERONOMY 26:11

Year 1

Year 2

Year 3

Year 4

Year 5

February 14

COLOR IS AN INBORN GIFT,
BUT APPRECIATION OF VALUE
IS MERELY TRAINING OF THE EYE,
WHICH EVERYONE OUGHT TO
BE ABLE TO ACQUIRE.

—JOHN SINGER SARGENT

Year 1

Year 2

Year 3

Year 4

Year 5

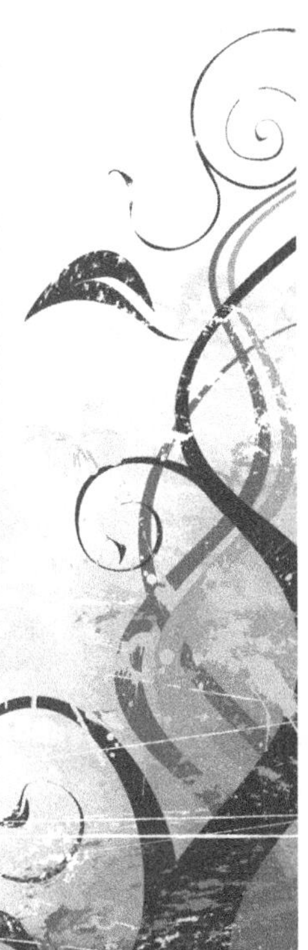

February 15

IN THE HOPES OF REACHING THE MOON
MEN FAIL TO SEE THE FLOWERS
THAT BLOSSOM AT THEIR FEET.

—ALBERT SCHWEITZER

Year 1

Year 2

Year 3

Year 4

Year 5

February 16

IF THE ONLY PRAYER YOU SAID
IN YOUR WHOLE LIFE WAS,
"THANK YOU,"
THAT WOULD SUFFICE.

—MEISTER ECKHART.

Year 1

Year 2

Year 3

Year 4

Year 5

February 17

BE THANKFUL. CULTIVATE AN "ATTITUDE OF GRATITUDE." THANKFULNESS IS MUCH MORE DEPENDENT ON ATTITUDE THAN CIRCUMSTANCE. WHEN YOU FEEL THE LACK OF WHAT YOU DON'T HAVE,

Year 1

Year 2

Year 3

Year 4

Year 5

February 18

THANK GOD FOR WHAT YOU DO HAVE! AT ANY TIME, THERE IS MORE GOING RIGHT IN THE LIFE OF A COMMITTED CHRISTIAN THAN THERE IS GOING WRONG. IT'S JUST THAT THE "WRONG" MAKES A LOT MORE NOISE THAN THE "RIGHT."

—JIM STEPHENS

Year 1

Year 2

Year 3

Year 4

Year 5

February 19

I THINK, WHAT HAS
THIS DAY BROUGHT ME,
AND WHAT HAVE I GIVEN IT?

—Henry Moore

Year 1

Year 2

Year 3

Year 4

Year 5

February 20

Now is no time to think of what you do not have. Think of what you can do with what there is.

—Ernest Hemingway

Year 1

Year 2

Year 3

Year 4

Year 5

February 21

HAPPINESS IS NOT ACHIEVED
BY THE CONSCIOUS PURSUIT
OF HAPPINESS; IT IS GENERALLY
THE BY-PRODUCT OF OTHER ACTIVITIES.

—ALDOUS HUXLEY

Year 1

Year 2

Year 3

Year 4

Year 5

February 22

DEFICIENCY MOTIVATION DOESN'T WORK.
IT WILL LEAD TO A LIFE-LONG
PURSUIT OF TRY TO FIX ME.
LEARN TO APPRECIATE WHAT YOU HAVE
AND WHERE AND WHO YOU ARE.

—WAYNE DYER

Year 1

Year 2

Year 3

Year 4

Year 5

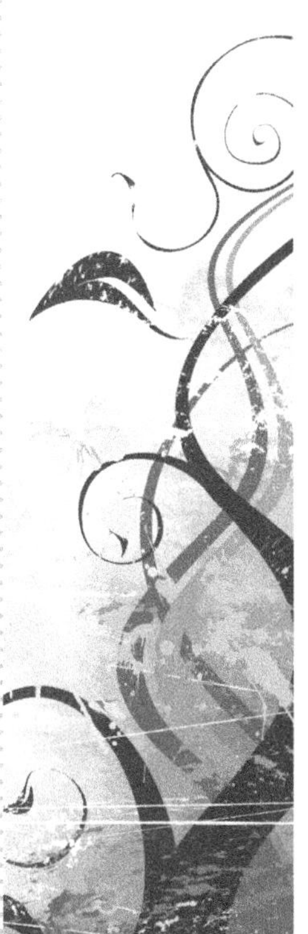

February 23

THERE IS MORE HUNGER FOR LOVE AND APPRECIATION IN THIS WORLD THAN FOR BREAD.

—MOTHER TERESA

Year 1

Year 2

Year 3

Year 4

Year 5

February 24

OUR DEEDS DETERMINE US, AS MUCH AS WE DETERMINE OUR DEEDS.

—GEORGE ELIOT

Year 1

Year 2

Year 3

Year 4

Year 5

February 25

I give thanks unto thee,
O Lord, and sing praises
unto thy name.

—Psalms

Year 1

Year 2

Year 3

Year 4

Year 5

THERE'S SOMETHING ABOUT DEATH
THAT IS COMFORTING.
THE THOUGHT THAT YOU COULD
DIE TOMORROW FREES YOU
TO APPRECIATE YOUR LIFE NOW.

—ANGELINA JOLIE

February 26

Year 1

Year 2

Year 3

Year 4

Year 5

February 27

WHO IS THE HAPPIEST OF MEN?
HE WHO VALUES THE MERITS OF OTHERS,
AND IN THEIR PLEASURE TAKES JOY,
EVEN AS THOUGH 'TWERE HIS OWN.

—JOHANN WOLFGANG VON GOETHE

Year 1

Year 2

Year 3

Year 4

Year 5

February 28

SILENT GRATITUDE
ISN'T MUCH USE TO ANYONE.

—GLADYS BERTHA STERN

Year 1

Year 2

Year 3

Year 4

Year 5

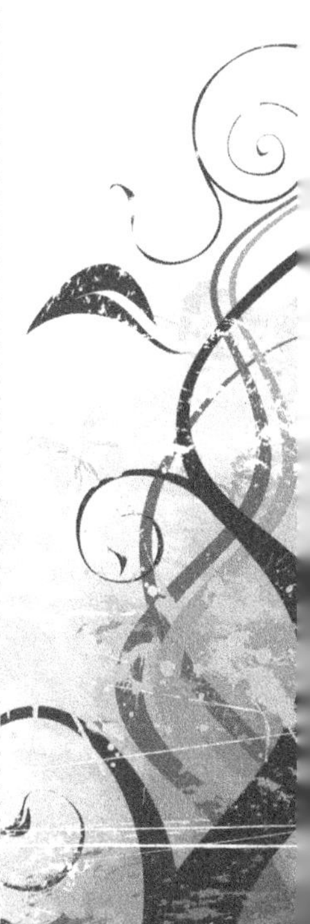

February 29

YOU HAVE IT EASILY IN YOUR POWER
TO INCREASE THE SUM TOTAL OF THIS
WORLD'S HAPPINESS NOW.
HOW? BY GIVING A FEW WORDS
OF SINCERE APPRECIATION TO SOMEONE

Leap Year

WHO IS LONELY OR DISCOURAGED. PERHAPS YOU WILL FORGET TOMORROW THE KIND WORDS YOU SAY TODAY, BUT THE RECIPIENT MAY CHERISH THEM OVER A LIFETIME.

—DALE CARNEGIE

March 1

Year 1

Year 2

Year 3

Year 4

Year 5

March 2

No duty is more urgent than that of returning thanks.

—Author unknown.

Year 1

Year 2

Year 3

Year 4

Year 5

March 3

We are so often caught up in our destination that we forget to appreciate the journey, especially the goodness of the people we meet on the way. Appreciation is a wonderful feeling, don't overlook it.

—Source Unknown

Year 1

Year 2

Year 3

Year 4

Year 5

March 4

EVERYDAY ENCHANTMENT CAN BE FOUND IN THE MOST ORDINARY OF PLACES.

—Deborah Norville

Year 1

Year 2

Year 3

Year 4

Year 5

March 5

BLESSED ARE THOSE THAT CAN GIVE WITHOUT REMEMBERING AND RECEIVE WITHOUT FORGETTING.

—AUTHOR UNKNOWN.

Year 1

Year 2

Year 3

Year 4

Year 5

March 6

PEOPLE MAY TAKE A JOB FOR MORE MONEY, BUT THEY OFTEN LEAVE IT FOR MORE RECOGNITION.

—BOB NELSON

Year 1

Year 2

Year 3

Year 4

Year 5

March 7

A PERSON STARTS TO LIVE
WHEN HE LIVES OUTSIDE HIMSELF.

—ALBERT SCHWEITZER

Year 1

Year 2

Year 3

Year 4

Year 5

March 8

Can you see the holiness in those things you take for granted—a paved road or a washing machine?

If you concentrate on finding whatever is good in every situation,

Year 1

Year 2

Year 3

Year 4

Year 5

YOU WILL DISCOVER THAT
YOUR LIFE WILL SUDDENLY BE FILLED
WITH GRATITUDE, A FEELING
THAT NURTURES THE SOUL.

—Rabbi Harold Kushner

March 9

Year 1

Year 2

Year 3

Year 4

Year 5

March 10

We count our miseries carefully, and accept our blessings without much thought.

—Chinese Proverb

Year 1

Year 2

Year 3

Year 4

Year 5

March 11

YOU SIMPLY WILL NOT BE THE SAME PERSON TWO MONTHS FROM NOW AFTER CONSCIOUSLY GIVING THANKS EACH DAY FOR THE ABUNDANCE THAT EXISTS IN YOUR LIFE. AND YOU WILL HAVE SET IN MOTION AN ANCIENT SPIRITUAL LAW: THE MORE YOU HAVE AND ARE GRATEFUL FOR, THE MORE WILL BE GIVEN YOU.

—SARAH BAN BREATHNACH, SIMPLE ABUNDANCE

Year 1

Year 2

Year 3

Year 4

Year 5

March 12

A WORD OF ENCOURAGEMENT DURING A FAILURE IS WORTH MORE THAN AN HOUR OF PRAISE AFTER SUCCESS.

—Anonymous

Year 1

Year 2

Year 3

Year 4

Year 5

March 13

GRATITUDE IS SOMETHING OF WHICH NONE OF US CAN GIVE TOO MUCH. FOR ON THE SMILES, THE THANKS WE GIVE, OUR LITTLE GESTURES OF APPRECIATION, OUR NEIGHBORS BUILD THEIR PHILOSOPHY OF LIFE.

—A. J. CRONIN

Year 1

Year 2

Year 3

Year 4

Year 5

March 14

Focus on a thing of beauty, and share it with someone else.

—Deborah Norville

Year 1

Year 2

Year 3

Year 4

Year 5

March 15

YOU CREATE THE EXPERIENCE OF LOVE BY GIVING THE GIFT OF ACCEPTANCE AND APPRECIATION.

—BILL FERGUSON

Year 1

Year 2

Year 3

Year 4

Year 5

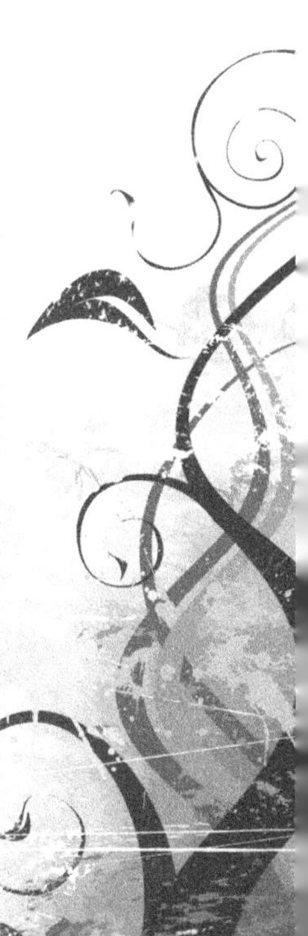

March 16

IF YOU DON'T START OUT
THE DAY WITH A SMILE,
IT'S NOT TOO LATE TO START
PRACTICING FOR TOMORROW.

—AUTHOR UNKNOWN

Year 1

Year 2

Year 3

Year 4

Year 5

March 17

IT IS NOT THE MAN
WHO HAS TOO LITTLE,
BUT THE MAN WHO CRAVES MORE,
THAT IS POOR.

—Seneca

Year 1

Year 2

Year 3

Year 4

Year 5

March 18

NOTHING IS MORE HONORABLE THAN A GRATEFUL HEART.

—SENECA

Year 1

Year 2

Year 3

Year 4

Year 5

Appreciation is a wonderful thing. It makes what is excellent in others belong to us as well.

—Voltaire

March 19

Year 1

Year 2

Year 3

Year 4

Year 5

March 20

TRUE THANKSGIVING MEANS THAT WE NEED TO THANK GOD FOR WHAT HE HAS DONE FOR US, AND NOT TO TELL HIM WHAT WE HAVE DONE FOR HIM.

—GEORGE R. HENDRICK

Year 1

Year 2

Year 3

Year 4

Year 5

March 21

DON'T OVERLOOK THE FAITHFUL CONSTANT BLESSINGS.

—AUTHOR UNKNOWN

Year 1

Year 2

Year 3

Year 4

Year 5

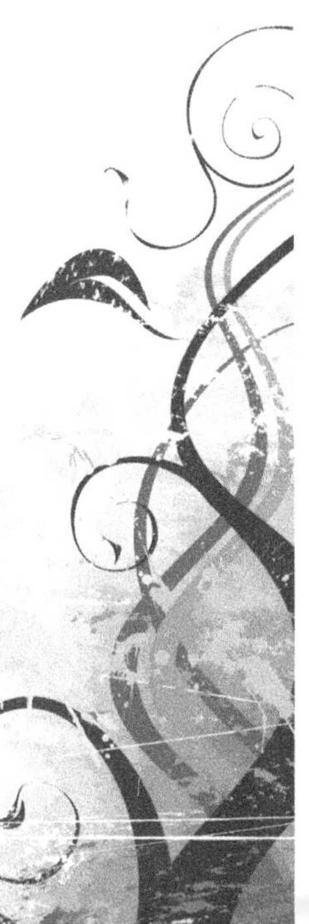

March 22

EACH DAY OFFERS US THE GIFT OF BEING A SPECIAL OCCASION IF WE CAN SIMPLY LEARN THAT AS WELL AS GIVING, IT IS BLESSED TO RECEIVE WITH GRACE AND A GRATEFUL HEART.

—SARAH BAN BREATHNACH

Year 1

Year 2

Year 3

Year 4

Year 5

THERE HAS NEVER BEEN ANOTHER YOU. WITH NO EFFORT ON YOUR PART YOU WERE BORN TO BE SOMETHING VERY SPECIAL AND SET APART. WHAT YOU ARE GOING TO DO IN APPRECIATION OF THAT GIFT IS A DECISION ONLY YOU CAN MAKE.

—DAN ZADRA

March 23

Year 1

Year 2

Year 3

Year 4

Year 5

March 24

A PLEASURE IS FULL GROWN ONLY WHEN IT IS REMEMBERED.

—C. S. Lewis

Year 1

Year 2

Year 3

Year 4

Year 5

March 25

GRATITUDE IS THE MEMORY OF THE HEART.

—FRENCH PROVERB

Year 1

Year 2

Year 3

Year 4

Year 5

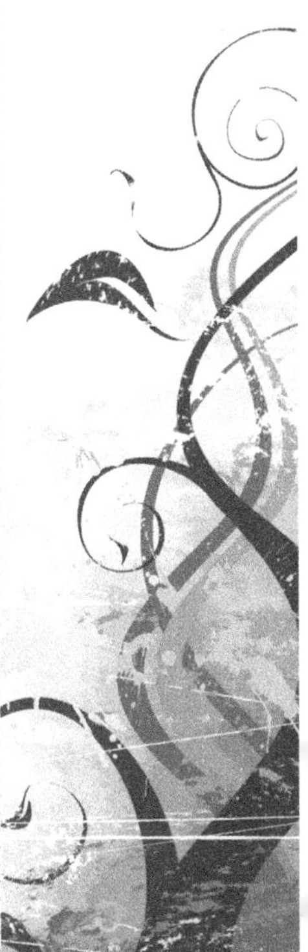

March 26

THERE IS NO DISASTER
THAT CAN'T BECOME A BLESSING.

—Richard Bach

Year 1

Year 2

Year 3

Year 4

Year 5

March 27

THE MORE ONE DOES AND SEES AND FEELS,
THE MORE ONE IS ABLE TO DO,
AND THE MORE GENUINE MAY BE ONE'S
APPRECIATION OF FUNDAMENTAL THINGS
LIKE HOME, AND LOVE,
AND UNDERSTANDING COMPANIONSHIP.

—AMELIA EARHART

Year 1

Year 2

Year 3

Year 4

Year 5

March 28

PEOPLE WILL FORGET WHAT YOU SAID,
THEY WILL FORGET WHAT YOU DID,
BUT THEY WILL NEVER FORGET
HOW YOU MAKE THEM FEEL.

—MAYA ANGELOU

Year 1

Year 2

Year 3

Year 4

Year 5

March 29

REFLECT ON YOUR PRESENT BLESSINGS—OF WHICH EVERY MAN HAS MANY—NOT ON YOUR PAST MISFORTUNES, OF WHICH ALL MEN HAVE SOME.

—CHARLES DICKENS

Year 1

Year 2

Year 3

Year 4

Year 5

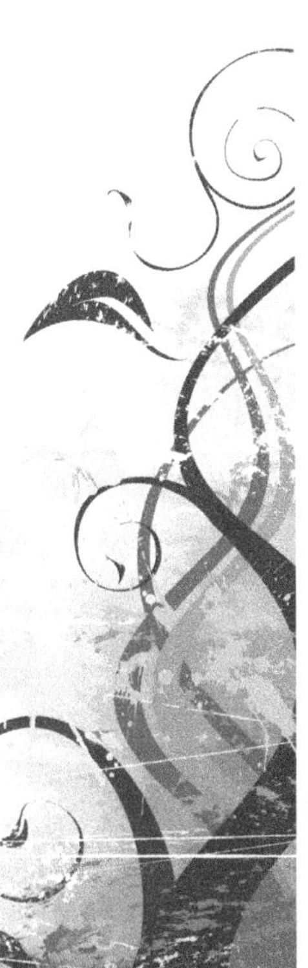

March 30

IN EVERY THING GIVE THANKS.

—1 Thessalonians 5:18

Year 1

Year 2

Year 3

Year 4

Year 5

March 31

BE GLAD OF LIFE,
BECAUSE IT GIVES YOU THE CHANCE
TO LIVE AND TO WORK AND TO PLAY
AND TO LOOK UP AT THE STARS.

—HENRY VAN DYKE

Year 1

Year 2

Year 3

Year 4

Year 5

Better to light a candle than to curse the darkness.

—Chinese Proverb

Year 1

Year 2

Year 3

Year 4

Year 5

April 2

DO NOT SAY, "IT IS MORNING," AND DISMISS IT WITH A NAME OF YESTERDAY. SEE IT FOR THE FIRST TIME AS A NEWBORN CHILD.

—RABINDRANATH TAGORE

Year 1

Year 2

Year 3

Year 4

Year 5

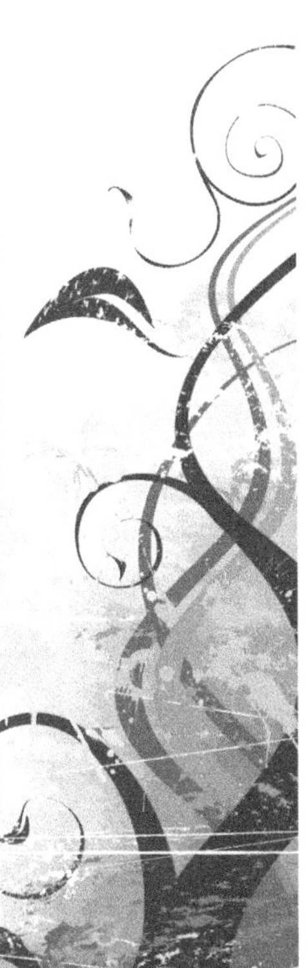

April 3

DON'T JUDGE EACH DAY
BY THE HARVEST YOU REAP,
BUT BY THE SEEDS YOU PLANT.

—ROBERT LOUIS STEVENSON

Year 1

Year 2

Year 3

Year 4

Year 5

April 4

Feeling gratitude and not expressing it is like wrapping a present and not giving it.

—William Arthur Ward

Year 1

Year 2

Year 3

Year 4

Year 5

April 5

At times our own light goes out and is rekindled by a spark from another person. Each of us has cause to think with deep gratitude of those who have lighted the flame within us.

—Albert Schweitzer

Year 1

Year 2

Year 3

Year 4

Year 5

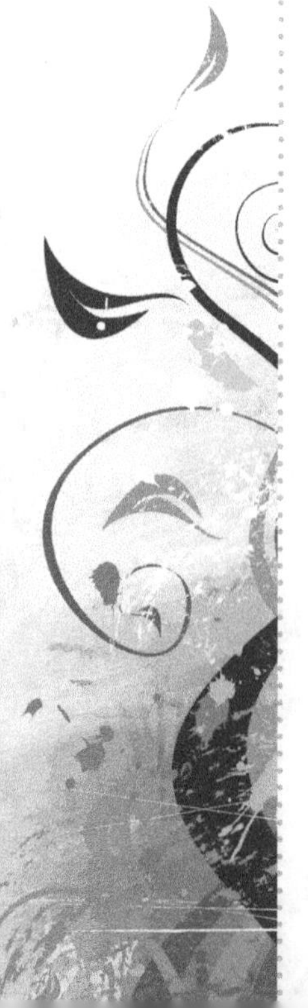

Correction does much,
but encouragement does more.
Encouragement after censure is as
the sun after a shower.

—Johann Wolfgang von Goethe

Year 1

Year 2

Year 3

Year 4

Year 5

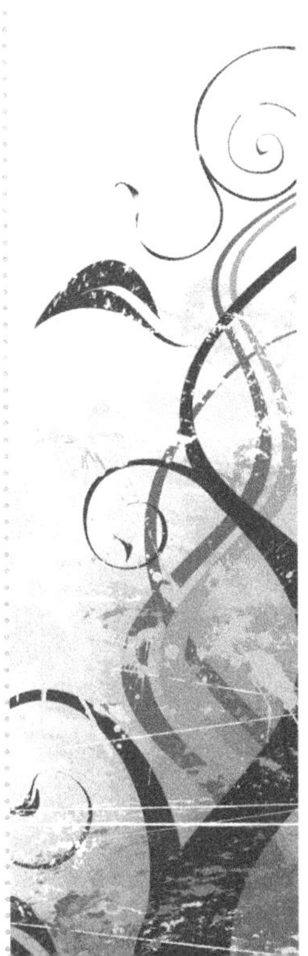

YOUR LIFE IS A REFLECTION
OF YOUR THOUGHTS.
IF YOU CHANGE YOUR THINKING,
YOU CHANGE YOUR LIFE.

—BRIAN TRACY

Year 1

Year 2

Year 3

Year 4

Year 5

April 8

GRATEFULNESS IS THE KEY TO A HAPPY LIFE THAT WE HOLD IN OUR HANDS, BECAUSE IF WE ARE NOT GRATEFUL, THEN NO MATTER HOW MUCH WE HAVE WE WILL NOT BE HAPPY—BECAUSE WE WILL ALWAYS WANT TO HAVE SOMETHING ELSE OR SOMETHING MORE.

—BROTHER DAVID STEINDL-RAST

Year 1

Year 2

Year 3

Year 4

Year 5

April 9

LET US RISE UP AND BE THANKFUL, FOR IF WE DIDN'T LEARN A LOT TODAY, AT LEAST WE LEARNED A LITTLE, AND IF WE DIDN'T LEARN A LITTLE, AT LEAST WE DIDN'T GET SICK, AND IF WE GOT SICK, AT LEAST WE DIDN'T DIE; SO, LET US ALL BE THANKFUL.

—BUDDHA

Year 1

Year 2

Year 3

Year 4

Year 5

NOR SHOULD THERE BE OBSCENITY,
FOOLISH TALK OR COARSE JOKING,
WHICH ARE OUT OF PLACE,
BUT RATHER THANKSGIVING.

—EPHESIANS 5:4

April 10

Year 1

Year 2

Year 3

Year 4

Year 5

April 11

COURTESIES OF A SMALL AND TRIVIAL CHARACTER ARE THE ONES WHICH STRIKE DEEPEST IN THE GRATEFULLY AND APPRECIATING HEART.

—HENRY CLAY

Year 1

Year 2

Year 3

Year 4

Year 5

You say grace before meals. All right. But I say grace before the concert and the opera, and grace before the play and pantomime, and grace before I open a book, and grace before sketching, painting, swimming, fencing, boxing, walking, playing, dancing and grace before I dip the pen in the ink.

—G. K. Chesterton

April 12

Year 1

Year 2

Year 3

Year 4

Year 5

April 13

ENCOURAGED PEOPLE ACHIEVE THE BEST; DOMINATED PEOPLE ACHIEVE SECOND BEST; NEGLECTED PEOPLE ACHIEVE THE LEAST.

—ANONYMOUS

Year 1

Year 2

Year 3

Year 4

Year 5

April 14

THERE IS NOTHING BETTER THAN THE ENCOURAGEMENT OF A GOOD FRIEND.

—JEAN JACQUES ROUSSEAU

Year 1

Year 2

Year 3

Year 4

Year 5

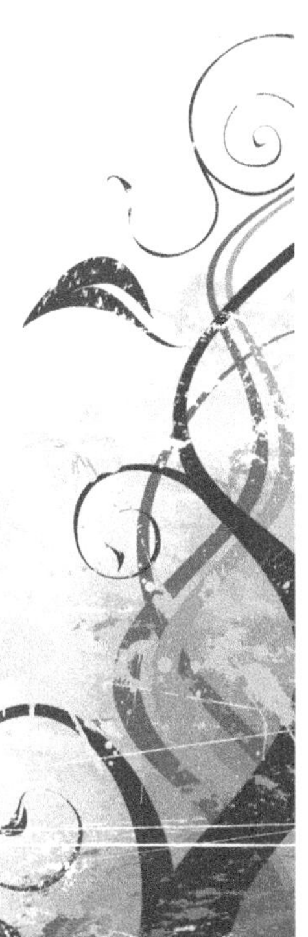

April 15

Gratitude unlocks the fullness of life. It turns what we have into enough, and more. It turns denial into acceptance, chaos into order, confusion into clarity....
It turns problems into gifts,

Year 1

Year 2

Year 3

Year 4

Year 5

FAILURES INTO SUCCESS, THE UNEXPECTED INTO PERFECT TIMING, AND MISTAKES INTO IMPORTANT EVENTS. GRATITUDE MAKES SENSE OF OUR PAST, BRINGS PEACE FOR TODAY AND CREATES A VISION FOR TOMORROW.

—MELODIE BEATTIE

April 16

Year 1

Year 2

Year 3

Year 4

Year 5

April 17

WHEN YOU ARE GRATEFUL FEAR DISAPPEARS AND ABUNDANCE APPEARS.

—ANTHONY ROBBINS

Year 1

Year 2

Year 3

Year 4

Year 5

April 18

OUR ENEMIES PROVIDE US WITH A PRECIOUS OPPORTUNITY TO PRACTICE PATIENCE AND LOVE. WE SHOULD HAVE GRATITUDE TOWARD THEM.

—TENZIN GYATSO THE 14TH DALAI LAMA

Year 1

Year 2

Year 3

Year 4

Year 5

April 19

Wake at dawn with a winged heart
and give thanks for
another day of loving.

—Kahlil Gibran

Year 1

Year 2

Year 3

Year 4

Year 5

April 20

GRATITUDE IS WHEN MEMORY IS STORED IN THE HEART AND NOT IN THE MIND.

—LIONEL HAMPTON

Year 1

Year 2

Year 3

Year 4

Year 5

April 21

GRATITUDE IS THE MOST EXQUISITE FORM OF COURTESY.

—JACQUES MARITAIN

Year 1

Year 2

Year 3

Year 4

Year 5

MOST OF US, SWIMMING AGAINST THE TIDES OF TROUBLE THE WORLD KNOWS NOTHING ABOUT, NEED ONLY A BIT OF PRAISE OR ENCOURAGEMENT— AND WE WILL MAKE THE GOAL.

—JEROME P. FLEISHMAN

April 22

Year 1

Year 2

Year 3

Year 4

Year 5

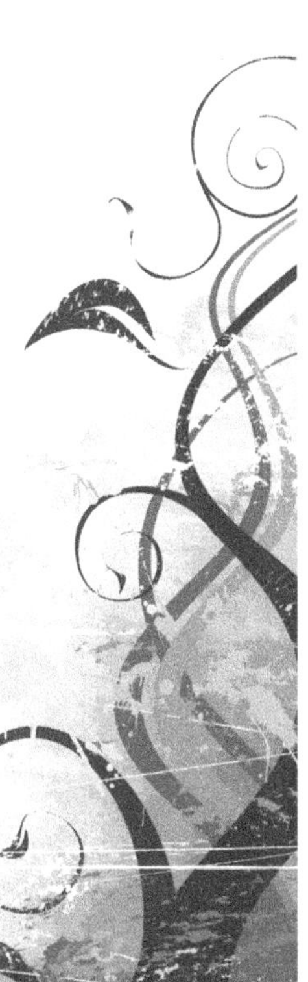

April 23

GOD GAVE YOU A GIFT OF
86,400 SECONDS TODAY.
HAVE YOU USED ONE TO SAY
"THANK YOU?"

—WILLIAM A. WARD

Year 1

Year 2

Year 3

Year 4

Year 5

April 24

Feeling grateful or appreciative of someone or something in your life actually attracts more of the things that you appreciate and value into your life.

—Christiane Northrup

Year 1

Year 2

Year 3

Year 4

Year 5

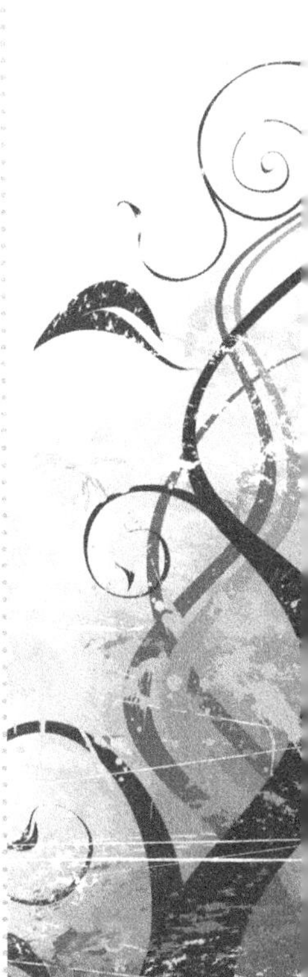

April 25

DEVELOP AN ATTITUDE OF GRATITUDE, AND GIVE THANKS FOR EVERYTHING THAT HAPPENS TO YOU, KNOWING THAT EVERY STEP FORWARD IS A STEP TOWARD ACHIEVING SOMETHING BIGGER AND BETTER THAN YOUR CURRENT SITUATION.

—BRIAN TRACY

Year 1

Year 2

Year 3

Year 4

Year 5

April 26

Be anxious for nothing,
but in everything by prayer
and supplication, with thanksgiving,
let your requests be made
known to God.

—Phil 4:6

Year 1

Year 2

Year 3

Year 4

Year 5

April 27

When a person doesn't have gratitude, something is missing in his or her humanity. A person can almost be defined by his or her attitude toward gratitude.

—Elie Wiesel, Holocaust survivor

Year 1

Year 2

Year 3

Year 4

Year 5

April 28

FIND THE GOOD—AND PRAISE IT.

—ALEX HALEY

Year 1

Year 2

Year 3

Year 4

Year 5

April 29

They are not poor that have little, but they that desire much. The richest man, whatever his lot, is the one who's content with his lot.

—Dutch Proverb

Year 1

Year 2

Year 3

Year 4

Year 5

April 30

Gratitude is our most direct line to God and the angels. If we take the time, no matter how crazy and troubled we feel, we can find something to be thankful for. The more we seek gratitude, the more reason the angels will give us for gratitude and joy to exist in our lives.

—Terry Lynn Taylor

Year 1

Year 2

Year 3

Year 4

Year 5

IF YOU CAN'T BE THANKFUL
FOR WHAT YOU RECEIVE,
BE THANKFUL FOR WHAT YOU ESCAPE.

—UNKNOWN

Year 1

Year 2

Year 3

Year 4

Year 5

May 2

GOD HAS TWO DWELLINGS;
ONE IN HEAVEN, AND THE OTHER
IN A MEEK AND THANKFUL HEART.

—IZAAK WALTON

Year 1

Year 2

Year 3

Year 4

Year 5

GRATITUDE IS A TWOFOLD LOVE—
LOVE COMING TO VISIT US,
AND LOVE RUNNING OUT
TO GREET A WELCOME GUEST.

—HENRY VAN DYKE

Year 1

Year 2

Year 3

Year 4

Year 5

May 4

THE BEST WAY TO PAY
FOR A LOVELY MOMENT
IS TO ENJOY IT.

—RICHARD BACH

Year 1

Year 2

Year 3

Year 4

Year 5

LIFE IS A PARADISE
FOR THOSE WHO LOVE
MANY THINGS
WITH A PASSION.

—LEO BUSCAGLIA

Year 1

Year 2

Year 3

Year 4

Year 5

May 6

I thank God for my handicaps for, through them, I have found myself, my work, and my God.

—Helen Keller

Year 1

Year 2

Year 3

Year 4

Year 5

BOTH ABUNDANCE AND LACK EXIST SIMULTANEOUSLY IN OUR LIVES, AS PARALLEL REALITIES. IT IS ALWAYS OUR CONSCIOUS CHOICE WHICH SECRET GARDEN WE WILL TEND... WHEN WE CHOOSE NOT TO FOCUS ON WHAT IS MISSING FROM OUR LIVES BUT ARE

Year 1

Year 2

Year 3

Year 4

Year 5

May 8

GRATEFUL FOR THE ABUNDANCE THAT'S PRESENT—LOVE, HEALTH, FAMILY, FRIENDS, WORK, THE JOYS OF NATURE AND PERSONAL PURSUITS THAT BRING US PLEASURE—THE WASTELAND OF ILLUSION FALLS AWAY AND WE EXPERIENCE HEAVEN ON EARTH.

—Sarah Ban Breathnach

Year 1

Year 2

Year 3

Year 4

Year 5

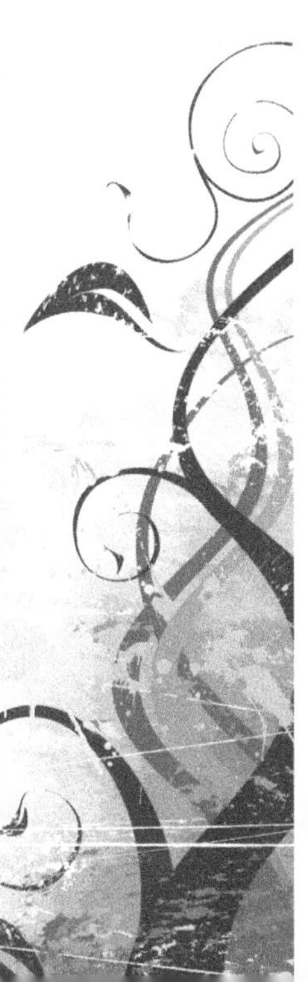

O LORD, WHO LENDS ME LIFE,
LEND ME A HEART REPLETE
WITH THANKFULNESS.

—WILLIAM SHAKESPEARE

Year 1

Year 2

Year 3

Year 4

Year 5

THE MOST FORTUNATE ARE THOSE WHO HAVE A WONDERFUL CAPACITY TO APPRECIATE AGAIN AND AGAIN, FRESHLY AND NAIVELY, THE BASIC GOODS OF LIFE, WITH AWE, PLEASURE, WONDER, AND EVEN ECSTASY.

—ABRAHAM MASLOW

May 10

Year 1

Year 2

Year 3

Year 4

Year 5

In our daily lives, we must see
that it is not happiness
that makes us grateful, but the
gratefulness that makes us happy.

—Albert Clarke

Year 1

Year 2

Year 3

Year 4

Year 5

There are only two ways
to live your life.
One is as though nothing
is a miracle.
The other is as though
everything is a miracle.

—Albert Einstein

Year 1

Year 2

Year 3

Year 4

Year 5

May 13

What if you gave someone a gift, and they neglected to thank you for it—would you be likely to give them another? Life is the same way. In order to attract more of the blessings that life has to offer, you must truly appreciate what you already have.

—Ralph Marston

Year 1

Year 2

Year 3

Year 4

Year 5

Whenever we are appreciative, we are filled with a sense of well-being and swept up by the feeling of joy.

—M. J. Ryan

May 14

Year 1

Year 2

Year 3

Year 4

Year 5

ALL MY LIFE THROUGH,
THE NEW SIGHTS OF NATURE
MADE ME REJOICE LIKE A CHILD.

—MADAME MARIE CURIE

Year 1

Year 2

Year 3

Year 4

Year 5

May 16

GRATITUDE IS RICHES.
COMPLAINT IS POVERTY.

—DORIS DAY

Year 1

Year 2

Year 3

Year 4

Year 5

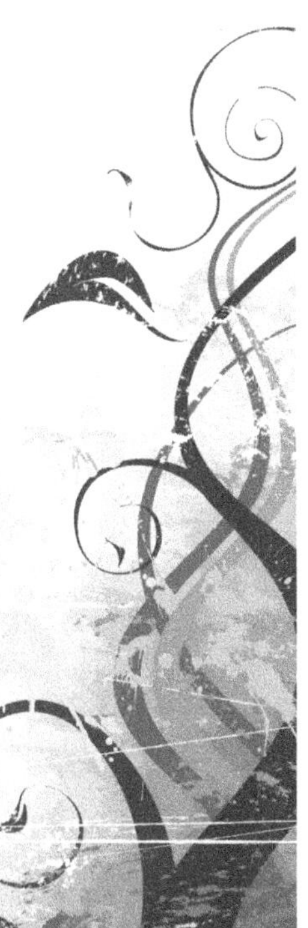

THERE ARE NO MISTAKES,
NO COINCIDENCES.
ALL EVENTS ARE BLESSINGS
GIVEN TO US TO LEARN FROM.

—ELISABETH KUBLER-ROSS

Year 1

Year 2

Year 3

Year 4

Year 5

May 18

I'M GRATEFUL FOR THE OPPORTUNITY TO LIVE ON THIS BEAUTIFUL AND ASTONISHING PLANET EARTH. IN THE MORNING, I WAKE UP WITH A SENSE OF GRATITUDE.

—EARL NIGHTINGALE

Year 1

Year 2

Year 3

Year 4

Year 5

Thankfulness is the beginning of gratitude. Gratitude is the completion of thankfulness. Thankfulness may consist merely of words. Gratitude is shown in acts.

—Henri Frederic Amiel

Year 1

Year 2

Year 3

Year 4

Year 5

May 20

APPRECIATE EVERYTHING YOUR ASSOCIATES DO FOR THE BUSINESS. NOTHING ELSE CAN QUITE SUBSTITUTE FOR A FEW WELL-CHOSEN, WELL-TIMED, SINCERE WORDS OF PRAISE. THEY'RE ABSOLUTELY FREE AND WORTH A FORTUNE.

—SAM WALTON

Year 1

Year 2

Year 3

Year 4

Year 5

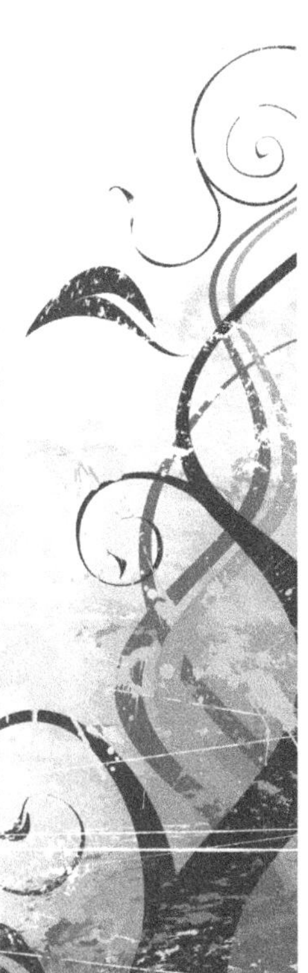

May 21

Life without thankfulness is devoid of love and passion. Hope without thankfulness is lacking in fine perception. Faith without thankfulness lacks strength and fortitude. Every virtue divorced from thankfulness is maimed and limps along the spiritual road.

—John Henry Jowett

Year 1

Year 2

Year 3

Year 4

Year 5

For each new morning with its light,
For rest and shelter of the night,
For health and food, for love
and friends, For everything
Thy goodness sends.

—Ralph Waldo Emerson

Year 1

Year 2

Year 3

Year 4

Year 5

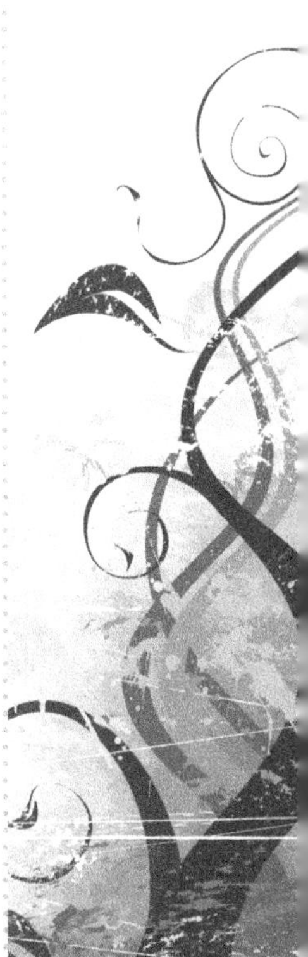

A GRATEFUL MIND IS A GREAT MIND WHICH EVENTUALLY ATTRACTS TO ITSELF GREAT THINGS.

—PLATO

Year 1

Year 2

Year 3

Year 4

Year 5

Some people grumble
because roses have thorns;
I am thankful that
the thorns have roses.

—Alphonse Karr

Year 1

Year 2

Year 3

Year 4

Year 5

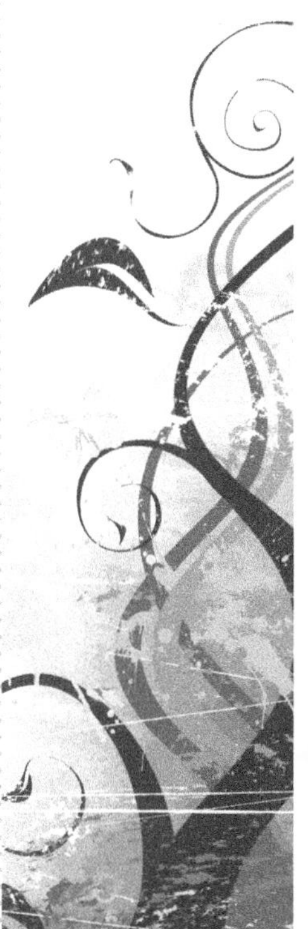

May 25

WHATEVER WE ARE WAITING FOR—PEACE OF MIND, CONTENTMENT, GRACE, THE INNER AWARENESS OF SIMPLE ABUNDANCE—IT WILL SURELY COME TO US, BUT ONLY WHEN WE ARE READY TO RECEIVE IT WITH AN OPEN AND GRATEFUL HEART.

—ELLEN VAUGHN

Year 1

Year 2

Year 3

Year 4

Year 5

HE WHO RECEIVES A GOOD TURN SHOULD NEVER FORGET IT; HE WHO DOES ONE SHOULD NEVER REMEMBER IT.

—PIERRE CHARRON

May 26

Year 1

Year 2

Year 3

Year 4

Year 5

May 27

MANY PEOPLE WHO ORDER
THEIR LIVES RIGHTLY IN ALL OTHER WAYS
ARE KEPT IN POVERTY BY
THEIR LACK OF GRATITUDE.

—WALLACE WATTLES

Year 1

Year 2

Year 3

Year 4

Year 5

May 28

I'd rather regret
the things that I have done
than the things that
I have not done.

—Lucille Ball

Year 1

Year 2

Year 3

Year 4

Year 5

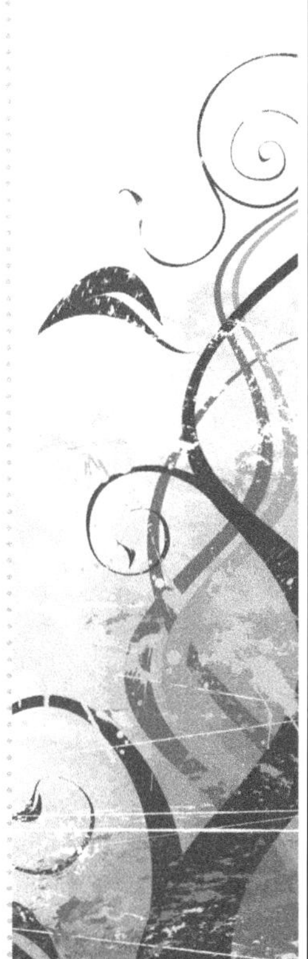

THE THANKFUL HEART IS ALWAYS CLOSE TO THE CREATIVE FORCES OF THE UNIVERSE, CAUSING COUNTLESS BLESSINGS TO FLOW TOWARD IT BY THE LAW OF RECIPROCAL RELATIONSHIP, BASED ON A COSMIC LAW OF ACTION AND REACTION.

—JOSEPH MURPHY

Year 1

Year 2

Year 3

Year 4

Year 5

May 30

EVERY MAN KNOWS THAT WHEN HIS WIFE IS APPRECIATING HIM FOR THE LITTLE THINGS THAT HE DOES, WHAT DOES HE WANT TO DO? HE WANTS TO DO MORE. IT'S ALWAYS ABOUT APPRECIATION.

—JOHN GRAY

Year 1

Year 2

Year 3

Year 4

Year 5

APPRECIATING THE GENIUS IN OTHERS ATTRACTS HIGH LEVELS OF COMPETENT ENERGY TO YOU. BY SEEING AND CELEBRATING THE CREATIVE GENIUS, YOU OPEN A CHANNEL WITHIN YOURSELF FOR RECEIVING THE CREATIVE ENERGY FROM THE FIELD OF INTENTION.

—WAYNE DYER

Year 1

Year 2

Year 3

Year 4

Year 5

June 1

GROW FLOWERS OF GRATITUDE
IN THE SOIL OF PRAYER.

—VERBENA WOODS

Year 1

Year 2

Year 3

Year 4

Year 5

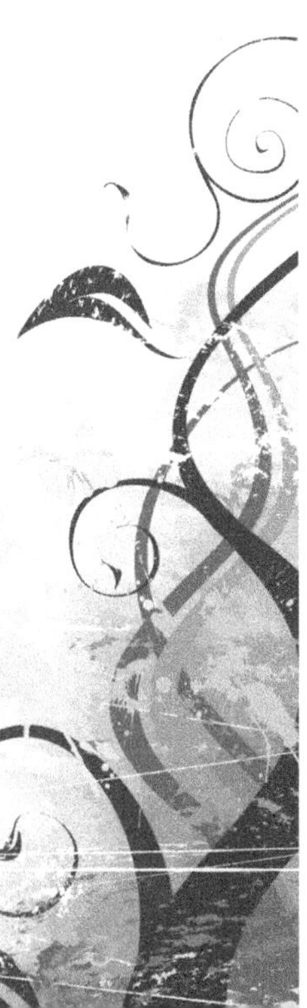

June 2

GRACE ISN'T A LITTLE PRAYER
YOU CHANT BEFORE RECEIVING A MEAL.
IT'S A WAY TO LIVE.

—JACKIE WINDSPEAR

Year 1

Year 2

Year 3

Year 4

Year 5

A noble person is mindful and thankful of the favors he receives from others.

—Buddha

June 3

Year 1

Year 2

Year 3

Year 4

Year 5

June 4

THE ESSENCE OF
ALL BEAUTIFUL ART,
ALL GREAT ART,
IS GRATITUDE.

—NIETZSCHE

Year 1

Year 2

Year 3

Year 4

Year 5

June 5

GRATITUDE INSULATES YOU FROM THE NEGATIVITY THAT OTHERS MAY WISH TO BRING INTO YOUR LIFE.

—AUTHOR UNKNOWN

Year 1

Year 2

Year 3

Year 4

Year 5

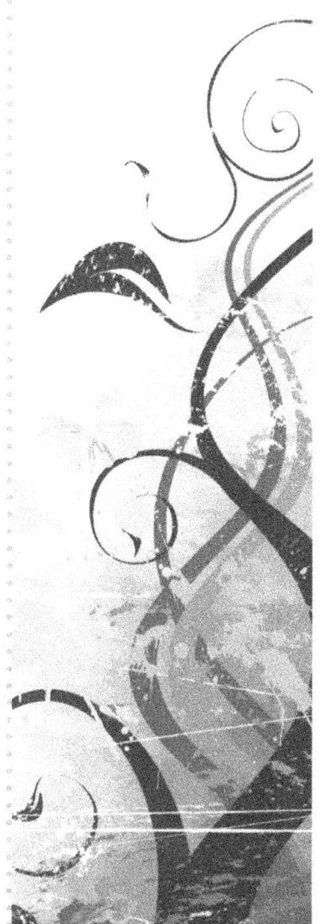

June 6

WE MAKE A LIVING
BY WHAT WE GET,
BUT WE MAKE A LIFE
BY WHAT WE GIVE.

—WINSTON CHURCHILL

Year 1

Year 2

Year 3

Year 4

Year 5

He is a wise man who does not grieve for the things which he has not, but rejoices in what he has.

—Epictetus

Year 1

Year 2

Year 3

Year 4

Year 5

June 8

CHEERFULNESS IS THE BEST PROMOTER OF HEALTH, AND IS AS FRIENDLY TO THE MIND AS TO THE BODY.

—JOSEPH ADDISON

Year 1

Year 2

Year 3

Year 4

Year 5

NO MATTER HOW MUCH APPRECIATION YOU GIVE, YOU'LL NEVER RUN OUT.

—AUTHOR UNKNOWN

Year 1

Year 2

Year 3

Year 4

Year 5

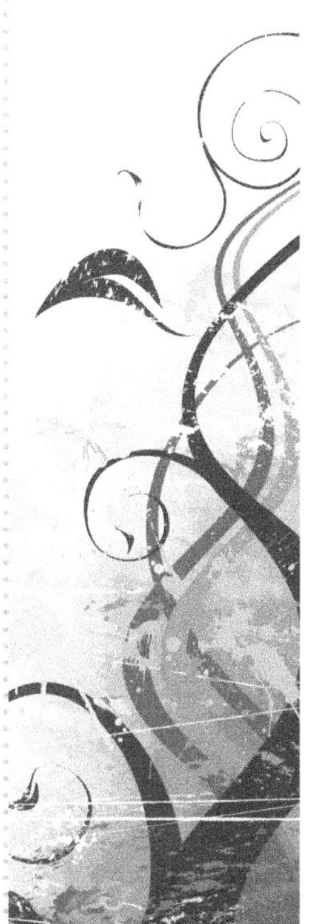

June 10

GRATITUDE IS THE BEST ATTITUDE.
THERE IS NOT A MORE PLEASING EXERCISE
OF THE MIND THAN GRATITUDE.
IT IS ACCOMPANIED WITH SUCH AN INWARD
SATISFACTION THAT THE DUTY IS SUFFICIENTLY
REWARDED BY THE PERFORMANCE.

—JOSEPH ADDISON

Year 1

Year 2

Year 3

Year 4

Year 5

WE OFTEN TAKE FOR GRANTED THE VERY THINGS THAT MOST DESERVE OUR GRATITUDE.

—CYNTHIA OZICK

June 11

Year 1

Year 2

Year 3

Year 4

Year 5

June 12

APPRECIATION IS A POWERFUL TOOL TO SHIFT PERSPECTIVE. FINDING SOMETHING TO APPRECIATE DURING A DIFFICULT SITUATION QUICKLY MOVES THE PERSPECTIVE TO THE BIG PICTURE FROM THE LITTLE PICTURE.

—DOC CHILDRE AND BRUCE CRYER, FROM CHAOS TO COHERENCE

Year 1

Year 2

Year 3

Year 4

Year 5

June 13

WHEN EATING BAMBOO SPROUTS,
REMEMBER THE MAN WHO PLANTED THEM.

—CHINESE PROVERB

Year 1

Year 2

Year 3

Year 4

Year 5

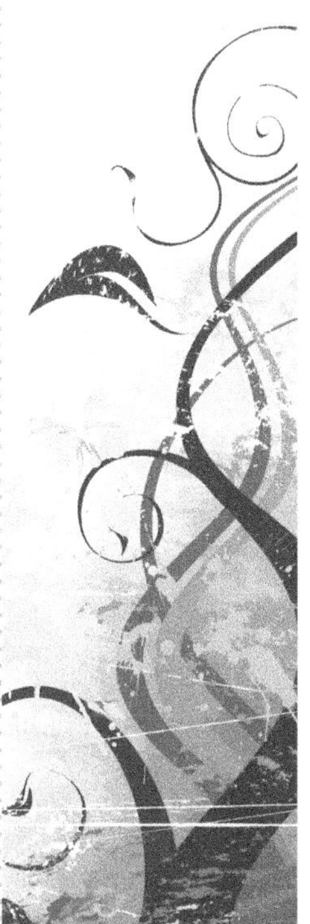

June 14

EACH DAY COMES BEARING
ITS OWN GIFTS. UNTIE THE RIBBONS.

—RUTH ANN SCHABACKER

Year 1

Year 2

Year 3

Year 4

Year 5

June 15

THE DIFFICULTIES, HARDSHIPS AND TRIALS OF LIFE, THE OBSTACLES... ARE POSITIVE BLESSINGS. THEY KNIT THE MUSCLES MORE FIRMLY, AND TEACH SELF-RELIANCE.

—William Matthews

Year 1

Year 2

Year 3

Year 4

Year 5

June 16

My advice to you is
not to inquire why or whither,
but just enjoy your ice cream
while it's on your plate.

—Thornton Wilder

Year 1

Year 2

Year 3

Year 4

Year 5

June 17

Sunshine is delicious,
rain is refreshing, wind braces us up,
snow is exhilarating; there is really
no such thing as bad weather, only
different kinds of good weather.

—John Ruskin

Year 1

Year 2

Year 3

Year 4

Year 5

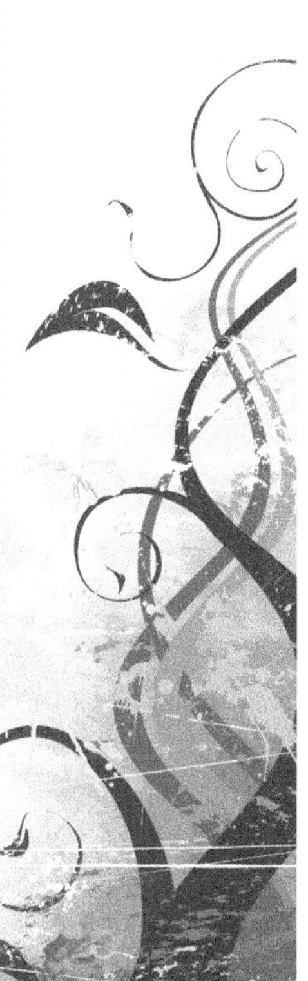

June 18

IF YOU WISH YOUR MERIT
TO BE KNOWN,
ACKNOWLEDGE THAT
OF OTHER PEOPLE.

—ORIENTAL PROVERB

Year 1

Year 2

Year 3

Year 4

Year 5

June 19

IF YOU WANT YOUR CHILDREN TO IMPROVE, LET THEM OVERHEAR THE NICE THINGS YOU SAY ABOUT THEM TO OTHERS.

—HAIM GINOTT

Year 1

Year 2

Year 3

Year 4

Year 5

June 20

IF ONLY PEOPLE WHO WORRY ABOUT THEIR LIABILITIES WOULD THINK ABOUT THE RICHES THEY DO POSSESS, THEY WOULD STOP WORRYING. WOULD YOU SELL BOTH YOUR EYES FOR A MILLION DOLLARS... OR YOUR TWO LEGS... OR YOUR HANDS...

Year 1

Year 2

Year 3

Year 4

Year 5

or your hearing? Add up what you do have, and you'll find that you won't sell them for all the gold in the world. The best things in life are yours, if you can appreciate yourself.

—Dale Carnegie

June 21

Year 1

Year 2

Year 3

Year 4

Year 5

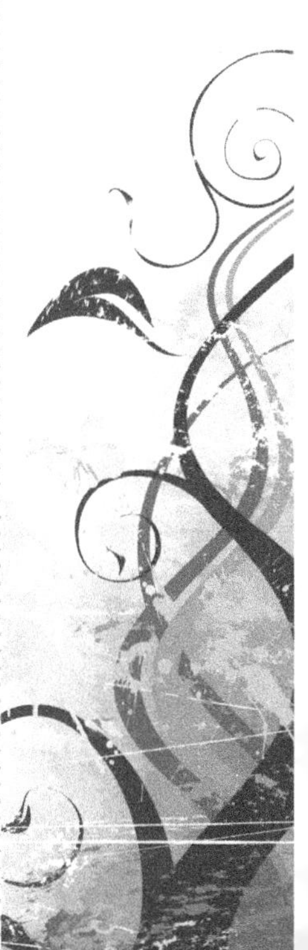

June 22

MOST OF US MISS OUT ON LIFE'S BIG PRIZES. THE PULITZER. THE NOBEL. OSCARS. TONYS. EMMYS. BUT WE'RE ALL ELIGIBLE FOR LIFE'S SMALL PLEASURES. A PAT ON THE BACK. A KISS BEHIND THE EAR. A FOUR-POUND BASS. A FULL MOON.

Year 1

Year 2

Year 3

Year 4

Year 5

June 23

An empty parking space. A crackling fire. A great meal. A glorious sunset. Hot soup. Cold beer. Don't fret about copping life's grand awards. Enjoy its tiny delights. There are plenty for all of us.

—United Technologies Corporation advertisement

Year 1

Year 2

Year 3

Year 4

Year 5

June 24

Nothing is more effective than sincere, accurate praise, and nothing is more lame than a cookie-cutter compliment.

—Bill Walsh

Year 1

Year 2

Year 3

Year 4

Year 5

LEARN EVERYTHING YOU CAN,
ANYTIME YOU CAN, FROM ANYONE
YOU CAN—THERE WILL ALWAYS
COME A TIME WHEN
YOU WILL BE GRATEFUL YOU DID.

—SARAH CALDWELL

Year 1

Year 2

Year 3

Year 4

Year 5

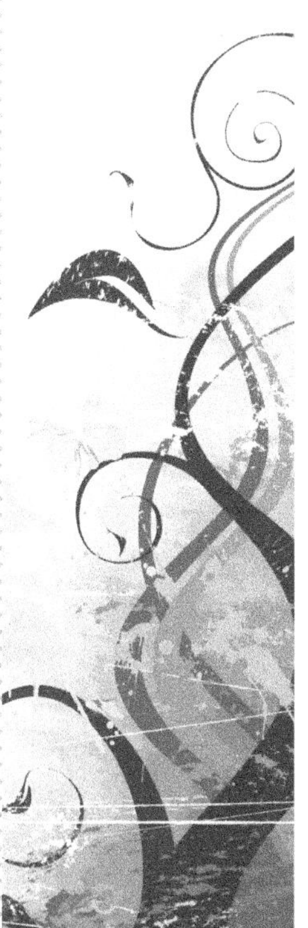

June 26

ROUGH DIAMONDS MAY SOMETIMES
BE MISTAKEN FOR WORTHLESS PEBBLES.

—SIR THOMAS BROWNE

Year 1

Year 2

Year 3

Year 4

Year 5

June 27

There but for the grace of God go I.

—Adam Applegarth

Year 1

Year 2

Year 3

Year 4

Year 5

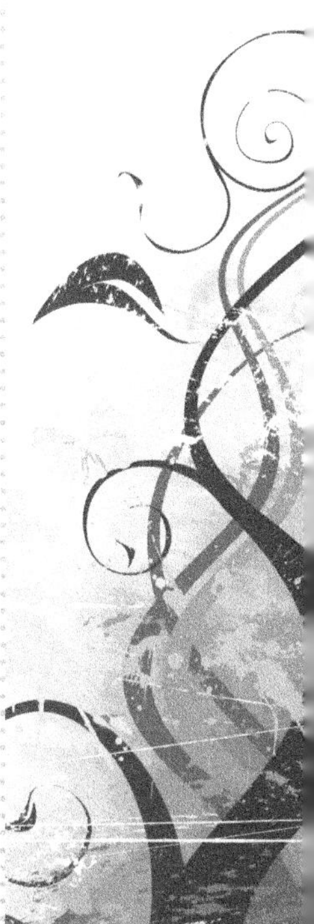

June 28

WHATEVER I AM OFFERED IN DEVOTION WITH A PURE HEART—A LEAF, A FLOWER, FRUIT, OR WATER—I ACCEPT WITH JOY.

—BHAGAVAD GITA

Year 1

Year 2

Year 3

Year 4

Year 5

A GRATEFUL PERSON TRUSTS ENOUGH
TO GIVE LIFE ANOTHER CHANCE,
TO STAY OPEN FOR SURPRISES.

—Brother David Steindal-Rast.

Year 1

Year 2

Year 3

Year 4

Year 5

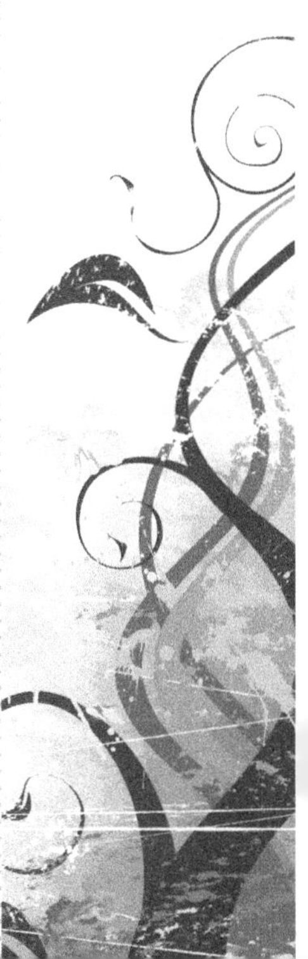

June 30

WHEN IT COMES TO LIFE
THE CRITICAL THING IS WHETHER
YOU TAKE THINGS FOR GRANTED OR
TAKE THEM WITH GRATITUDE.

—G. K. CHESTERTON

Year 1

Year 2

Year 3

Year 4

Year 5

PROMISE YOURSELF
TO BE JUST AS ENTHUSIASTIC
ABOUT THE SUCCESS OF OTHERS
AS YOU ARE ABOUT YOUR OWN.

—CHRISTIAN LARSON

Year 1

Year 2

Year 3

Year 4

Year 5

MANY PEOPLE ARE UNDONE BY CRISIS.
GRATEFUL PEOPLE AREN'T.

—DEBORAH NORVILLE

Year 1

Year 2

Year 3

Year 4

Year 5

THERE ARE REALITIES WE ALL SHARE, REGARDLESS OF OUR NATIONALITY, LANGUAGE, OR INDIVIDUAL TASTES. AS WE NEED FOOD, SO DO WE NEED EMOTIONAL NOURISHMENT: LOVE, KINDNESS, APPRECIATION, AND SUPPORT FROM OTHERS.

—J. DONALD WALTERS

Year 1

Year 2

Year 3

Year 4

Year 5

THOSE WHO BRING SUNSHINE
TO THE LIVES OF OTHERS
CANNOT KEEP IT FROM THEMSELVES.

—JAMES M. BARRIE

Year 1

Year 2

Year 3

Year 4

Year 5

July 5

YOU NEED TO BE AWARE OF WHAT OTHERS ARE DOING, APPLAUD THEIR EFFORTS, ACKNOWLEDGE THEIR SUCCESSES, AND ENCOURAGE THEM IN THEIR PURSUITS. WHEN WE ALL HELP ONE ANOTHER, EVERYBODY WINS.

—JIM STOVALL

Year 1

Year 2

Year 3

Year 4

Year 5

WHEN ANY... ACT OF CHARITY OR OF GRATITUDE, FOR INSTANCE, IS PRESENTED TO OUR SIGHT OR IMAGINATION, WE ARE DEEPLY IMPRESSED WITH ITS BEAUTY AND FEEL A STRONG DESIRE IN OURSELVES OF DOING CHARITABLE AND GRATEFUL ACTS ALSO.

—THOMAS JEFFERSON IN A 1771 LETTER

Year 1

Year 2

Year 3

Year 4

Year 5

If you want to lift yourself up,
lift up someone else.

—Booker T. Washington

Year 1

Year 2

Year 3

Year 4

Year 5

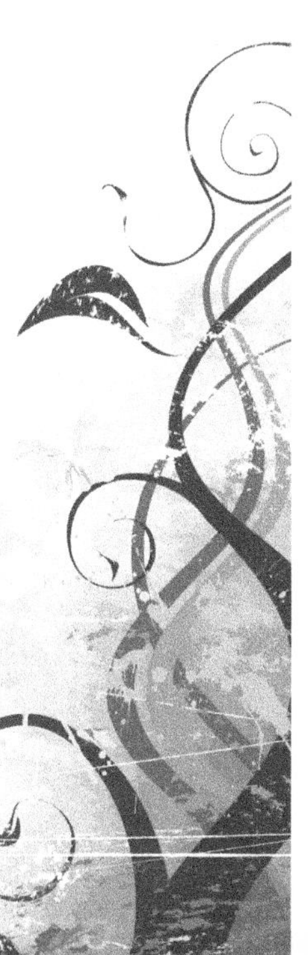

Until you value yourself,
you will not value your time.
Until you value your time,
you will not do anything with it.

—M. Scott Peck

Year 1

Year 2

Year 3

Year 4

Year 5

I HAVE LEARNED TO BE CONTENT IN WHATEVER CIRCUMSTANCES I AM.

—PHILLIPIANS 4:11

Year 1

Year 2

Year 3

Year 4

Year 5

WHEN OTHER PEOPLE ARE MADE TO FEEL IMPORTANT AND APPRECIATED, IT WILL NO LONGER BE NECESSARY FOR THEM TO WHITTLE OTHERS DOWN IN ORDER TO BE SEEN BIGGER BY COMPARISON.

—VIRGINIA ARCASTLE

Year 1

Year 2

Year 3

Year 4

Year 5

It is amazing what you can accomplish if you do not care who gets the credit.

—Harry Truman

Year 1

Year 2

Year 3

Year 4

Year 5

July 12

WE HAVE NO RIGHT TO ASK
WHEN A SORROW COMES,
"WHY DID THIS HAPPEN TO ME?"
UNLESS WE ASK THE SAME QUESTION
FOR EVERY JOY THAT COMES OUR WAY.

—FREDERICK KEONIG

Year 1

Year 2

Year 3

Year 4

Year 5

THE THANKFUL RECEIVER BEARS A PLENTIFUL HARVEST.

—William Blake

July 13

Year 1

Year 2

Year 3

Year 4

Year 5

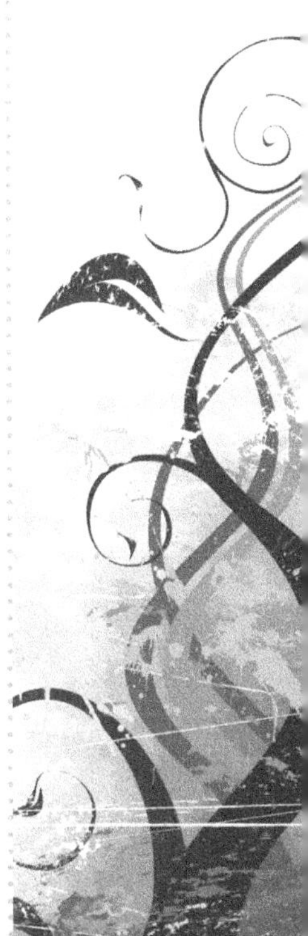

THERE IS A CALMNESS
TO A LIFE LIVED IN GRATITUDE,
A QUIET JOY.

—RALPH H. BLUM

Year 1

Year 2

Year 3

Year 4

Year 5

July 15

Two kinds of gratitude:
the sudden kind we feel
for what we take; the larger kind
we feel for what we give.

—Edward Arlington Robinson

Year 1

Year 2

Year 3

Year 4

Year 5

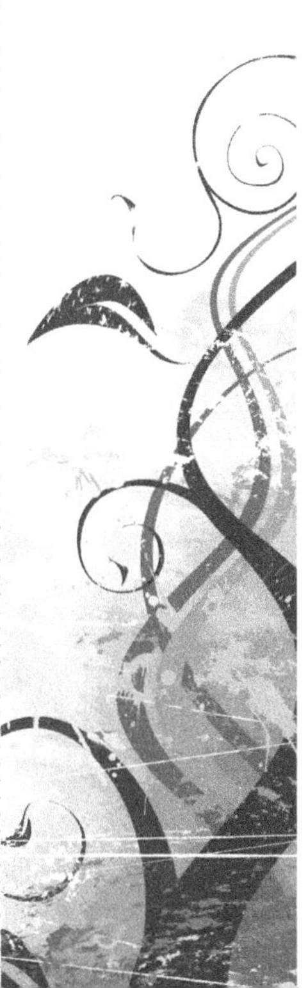

July 16

Life is huge! Rejoice about the sun, moon, flowers, and sky. Rejoice about the food you have to eat. Rejoice about the body that houses your spirit. Rejoice about the fact that you

Year 1

Year 2

Year 3

Year 4

Year 5

CAN BE A POSITIVE FORCE IN THE WORLD AROUND YOU. REJOICE ABOUT THE LOVE THAT IS AROUND YOU. IF YOU WANT TO BE HAPPY, COMMIT TO MAKING YOUR LIFE ONE OF REJOICING.

—AUTHOR UNKNOWN

July 17

Year 1

Year 2

Year 3

Year 4

Year 5

A maxim is the exact and noble expression of an important and indisputable truth. Good maxims are the germs of all excellence; when firmly fixed on the memory, they nourish the will.

—Joseph Joubert

Year 1

Year 2

Year 3

Year 4

Year 5

THERE'S NOTHING GREATER IN THE WORLD THAN WHEN SOMEBODY ON THE TEAM DOES SOMETHING GOOD, AND EVERYBODY GATHERS AROUND TO PAT HIM ON THE BACK.

—BILLY MARTIN

July 19

Year 1

Year 2

Year 3

Year 4

Year 5

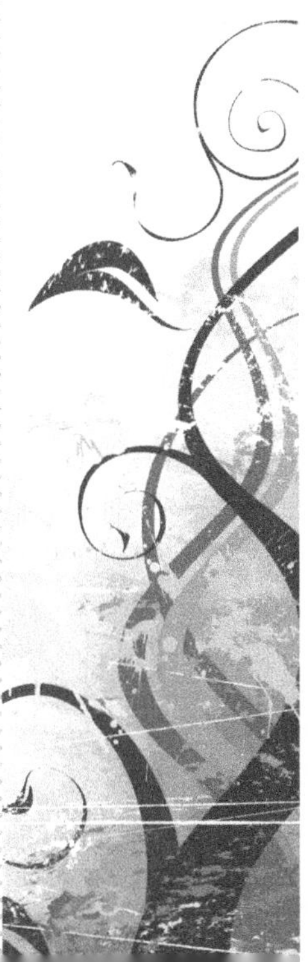

MAKE IT A HABIT TO TELL PEOPLE THANK YOU. TO EXPRESS YOUR APPRECIATION, SINCERELY AND WITHOUT THE EXPECTATION OF ANYTHING IN RETURN. TRULY APPRECIATE THOSE

Year 1

Year 2

Year 3

Year 4

Year 5

AROUND YOU, AND YOU'LL SOON FIND MANY OTHERS AROUND YOU. TRULY APPRECIATE LIFE, AND YOU'LL FIND THAT YOU HAVE MORE OF IT.

—Ralph Marston

July 21

Year 1

Year 2

Year 3

Year 4

Year 5

THAT A MAN IS SUCCESSFUL WHO HAS LIVED WELL, LAUGHED OFTEN, AND LOVED MUCH, WHO HAS GAINED THE RESPECT OF THE INTELLIGENT MEN AND THE LOVE OF CHILDREN; WHO HAS FILLED HIS NICHE AND ACCOMPLISHED HIS TASK; WHO LEAVES THE WORLD BETTER THAN HE

Year 1

Year 2

Year 3

Year 4

Year 5

July 23

FOUND IT, WHETHER BY AN IMPROVED POPPY, A PERFECT POEM, OR A RESCUED SOUL; WHO NEVER LACKED APPRECIATION OF EARTH'S BEAUTY OR FAILED TO EXPRESS IT; WHO LOOKED FOR THE BEST IN OTHERS AND GAVE THE BEST HE HAD.

—Robert Louis Stevenson

Year 1

Year 2

Year 3

Year 4

Year 5

THE BEST WAY TO APPRECIATE YOUR JOB IS TO IMAGINE YOURSELF WITHOUT ONE.

—Oscar Wilde

Year 1

Year 2

Year 3

Year 4

Year 5

IF YOU SEE NO REASON FOR GIVING THANKS, THE FAULT LIES IN YOURSELF.

—MINQUASS AMERICAN INDIAN SAYING

July 25

Year 1

Year 2

Year 3

Year 4

Year 5

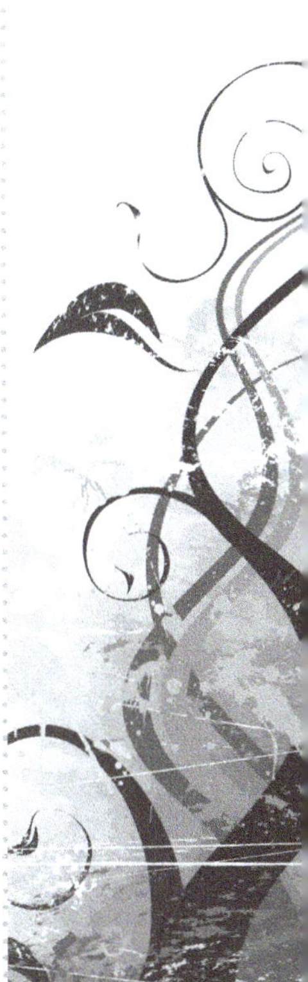

REAL LIFE ISN'T ALWAYS GOING
TO BE PERFECT OR GO OUR WAY,
BUT THE RECURRING ACKNOWLEDGMENT
OF WHAT IS WORKING IN OUR LIVES CAN
HELP US NOT ONLY TO SURVIVE
BUT SURMOUNT OUR DIFFICULTIES.

—SARAH BAN BREATHNACH

Year 1

Year 2

Year 3

Year 4

Year 5

July 27

NEXT TO EXCELLENCE IS THE APPRECIATION OF IT.

—WILLIAM MAKEPEACE

Year 1

Year 2

Year 3

Year 4

Year 5

APPRECIATION OF LIFE ITSELF, BECOMING SUDDENLY AWARE OF THE MIRACLE OF BEING ALIVE, ON THIS PLANET, CAN TURN WHAT WE CALL ORDINARY LIFE INTO A MIRACLE.

—DAN WAKEFIELD

Year 1

Year 2

Year 3

Year 4

Year 5

July 29

Be thankful for what you have
and you will end up having more.
But if you concentrate on
what you don't have,
you'll never, ever have enough.

—Oprah Winfrey

Year 1

Year 2

Year 3

Year 4

Year 5

WHEN THE HEART
IS FULL OF GRATITUDE,
THERE IS LITTLE ROOM
LEFT FOR DESPAIR.

—ST. PAUL

Year 1

Year 2

Year 3

Year 4

Year 5

Gratitude helps you to grow and expand; gratitude brings joy and laughter into your life and into the lives of all those around you.

—Eileen Caddy

July 31

Year 1

Year 2

Year 3

Year 4

Year 5

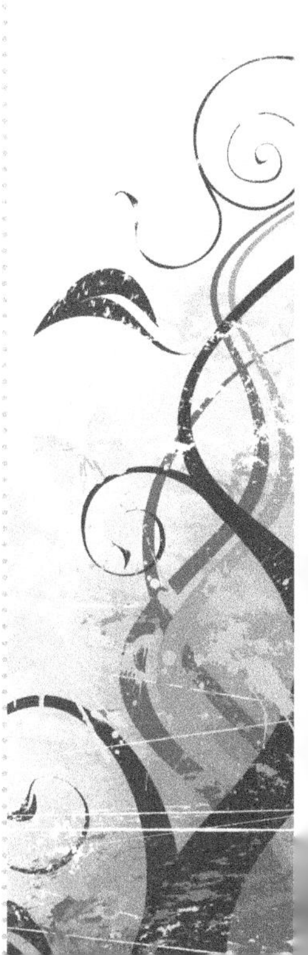

August 1

TREAT PEOPLE AS IF THEY WERE WHAT THEY OUGHT TO BE AND YOU HELP THEM TO BECOME WHAT THEY ARE CAPABLE OF BEING.

—JOHANN WOLFGANG VON GOETHE

Year 1

Year 2

Year 3

Year 4

Year 5

August 2

DON'T TELL GOD HOW BIG YOUR STORM IS, TELL THE STORM HOW BIG YOUR GOD IS.

—AUTHOR UNKNOWN

Year 1

Year 2

Year 3

Year 4

Year 5

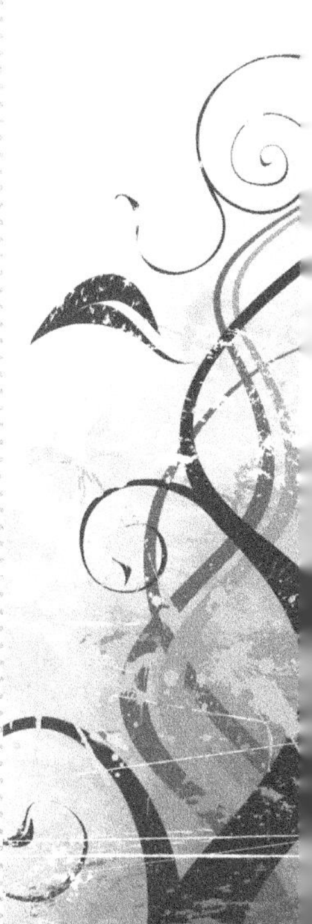

August 3

WE OFTEN TAKE FOR GRANTED THE VERY THINGS THAT MOST DESERVE OUR GRATITUDE.

—CYNTHIA OZICK

Year 1

Year 2

Year 3

Year 4

Year 5

August 4

GRATITUDE IS THE SIGN OF NOBLE SOULS.

—AESOP

Year 1

Year 2

Year 3

Year 4

Year 5

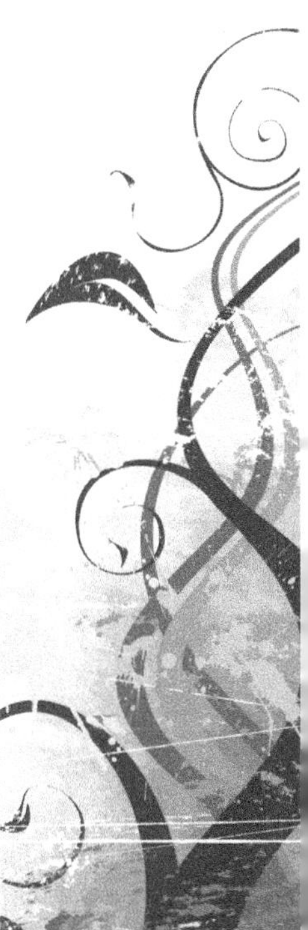

August 5

NOTHING ON EARTH CAN STOP THE MAN WITH THE RIGHT MENTAL ATTITUDE FROM ACHIEVING HIS GOAL; NOTHING ON EARTH CAN HELP THE MAN WITH THE WRONG MENTAL ATTITUDE.

—THOMAS JEFFERSON

Year 1

Year 2

Year 3

Year 4

Year 5

August 6

HAPPINESS IS A BY-PRODUCT
OF AN EFFORT TO
MAKE SOMEONE ELSE HAPPY.

—GRETTA PALMER

Year 1

Year 2

Year 3

Year 4

Year 5

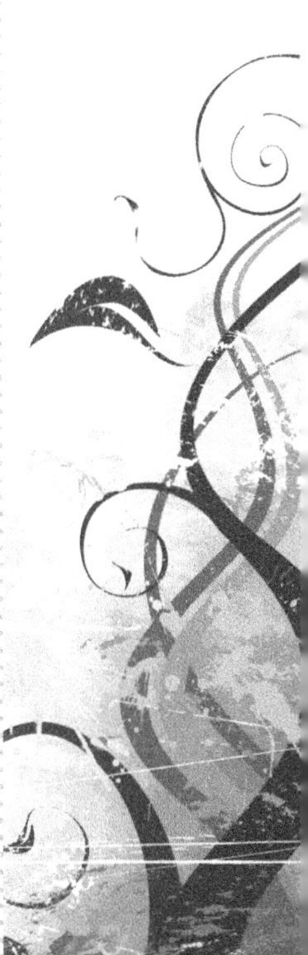

August 7

APPRECIATING EACH OTHER IS A TRUE FAMILY VALUE, ONE THAT WILL BAIL OUT MUCH OF THE STRESS ON THE PLANET AND HELP STRENGTHEN THE UNIVERSAL BOND ALL PEOPLE HAVE.

—SARA PADDISON, HIDDEN POWER OF THE HEART

Year 1

Year 2

Year 3

Year 4

Year 5

August 8

Gratitude for the abundance
you have received
is the best insurance that
the abundance will continue.

—Muhammad

Year 1

Year 2

Year 3

Year 4

Year 5

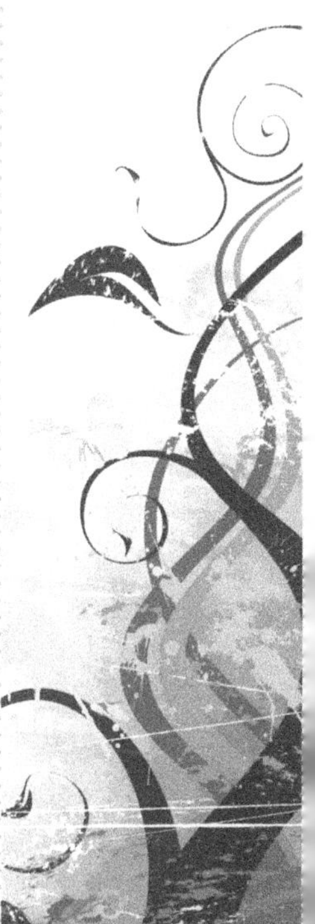

August 9

WE TEND TO FORGET THAT
HAPPINESS DOESN'T COME AS A RESULT
OF GETTING SOMETHING WE DON'T HAVE,
BUT RATHER OF RECOGNIZING AND
APPRECIATING WHAT WE DO HAVE.

—FREDERICK KEONIG

Year 1

Year 2

Year 3

Year 4

Year 5

August 10

IF YOU CAN READ THIS,
THANK A TEACHER.

—AUTHOR UNKNOWN

Year 1

Year 2

Year 3

Year 4

Year 5

August 11

ANY MAN'S LIFE WILL BE FILLED WITH CONSTANT AND UNEXPECTED ENCOURAGEMENT IF HE MAKES UP HIS MIND TO DO HIS LEVEL BEST EACH DAY.

—BOOKER T. WASHINGTON

Year 1

Year 2

Year 3

Year 4

Year 5

August 12

THE GREATEST HUMILIATION IN LIFE IS TO WORK HARD ON SOMETHING FROM WHICH YOU EXPECT GREAT APPRECIATION, AND THEN FAIL TO GET IT.

—EDGAR WATSON HOWE

Year 1

Year 2

Year 3

Year 4

Year 5

August 13

The spirited horse,
which will try to win
the race of its own accord,
will run even faster
if encouraged.

—Ovid

Year 1

Year 2

Year 3

Year 4

Year 5

THOSE WHO ARE LIFTING
THE WORLD UPWARD AND ONWARD
ARE THOSE WHO ENCOURAGE
MORE THAN CRITICIZE.

—ELIZABETH HARRISON

Year 1

Year 2

Year 3

Year 4

Year 5

August 15

Pretend that every single person you meet has a sign around his or her neck that says, Make Me Feel Important. Not only will you succeed in sales, you will succeed in life.

—Mary Kay Ash

Year 1

Year 2

Year 3

Year 4

Year 5

THE AIM OF LIFE IS APPRECIATION; THERE IS NO SENSE IN NOT APPRECIATING THINGS; AND THERE IS NO SENSE IN HAVING MORE OF THEM IF YOU HAVE LESS APPRECIATION OF THEM.

—GILBERT K. CHESTERTON

August 16

Year 1

Year 2

Year 3

Year 4

Year 5

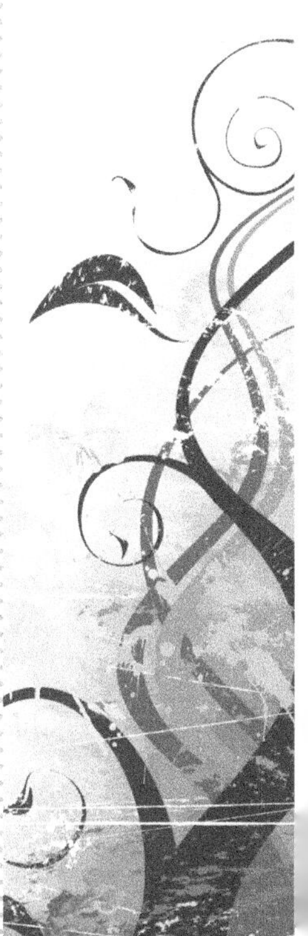

August 17

IN ORDINARY LIFE WE
HARDLY REALIZE THAT WE RECEIVE
A GREAT DEAL MORE THAN WE GIVE,
AND THAT IT IS ONLY WITH GRATITUDE
THAT LIFE BECOMES RICH.

—DIETRICH BONHOEFFER

Year 1

Year 2

Year 3

Year 4

Year 5

I WOULD MAINTAIN THAT THANKS ARE THE HIGHEST FORM OF THOUGHT, AND THAT GRATITUDE IS HAPPINESS DOUBLED BY WONDER.

—G. K. CHESTERTON

August 18

Year 1

Year 2

Year 3

Year 4

Year 5

August 19

MOST PEOPLE DO NOT RECEIVE
NEARLY ENOUGH APPRECIATION.
HOW CAN THIS BE WHEN APPRECIATION
IS FREE, EASY, AND READILY AVAILABLE?
ALL YOU HAVE TO DO IS SPEAK.
GO GIVE SOME AWAY NOW.

—RHOBERTA SHALER PHD

Year 1

Year 2

Year 3

Year 4

Year 5

August 20

THE TALENT FOR BEING HAPPY IS APPRECIATING AND LIKING WHAT YOU HAVE, INSTEAD OF WHAT YOU DON'T HAVE.

—WOODY ALLEN

Year 1

Year 2

Year 3

Year 4

Year 5

IF YOU DON'T APPRECIATE IT,
YOU DON'T DESERVE IT.
—TERRY JOSEPHSON

Year 1

Year 2

Year 3

Year 4

Year 5

August 22

SILENT GRATITUDE
ISN'T VERY MUCH USE TO ANYONE.

—GERTRUDE STEIN

Year 1

Year 2

Year 3

Year 4

Year 5

August 23

GRATITUDE BESTOWS REVERENCE,
ALLOWING US TO ENCOUNTER
EVERYDAY EPIPHANIES,
THOSE TRANSCENDENT MOMENTS
OF AWE THAT CHANGE FOREVER HOW
WE EXPERIENCE LIFE AND THE WORLD.

—JOHN MILTON

Year 1

Year 2

Year 3

Year 4

Year 5

August 24

THERE ARE FEW FINER EXCESSES IN THE WORLD THAN AN EXCESS OF GRATITUDE.

—JEAN DE LA BRUYERE

Year 1

Year 2

Year 3

Year 4

Year 5

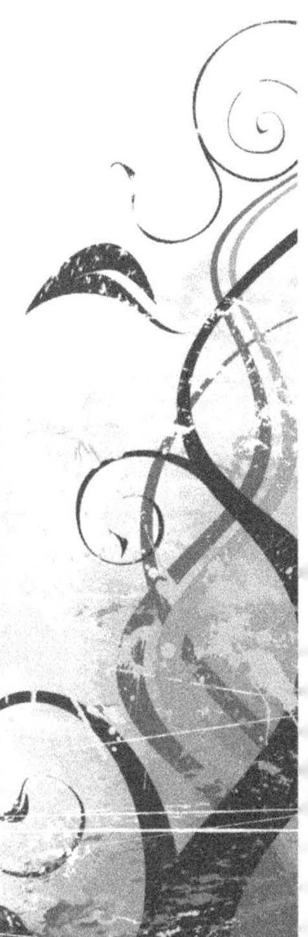

August 25

WHAT LIES BEHIND US
AND WHAT LIES BEFORE US
ARE TINY MATTERS COMPARED
TO WHAT LIES WITHIN US.

—RALPH WALDO EMERSON

Year 1

Year 2

Year 3

Year 4

Year 5

August 26

LIFE IS A GIFT.
OPEN YOUR PRESENT.

—RAIN BOJANGLES

Year 1

Year 2

Year 3

Year 4

Year 5

August 27

When I first open my eyes
upon the morning meadows
and look out upon
the beautiful world,
I thank God I am alive.

—Ralph Waldo Emerson

Year 1

Year 2

Year 3

Year 4

Year 5

August 28

Be an angel to someone else
whenever you can,
as a way of thanking God
for the help your angel
has given you.

—Eileen Elias Freeman

Year 1

Year 2

Year 3

Year 4

Year 5

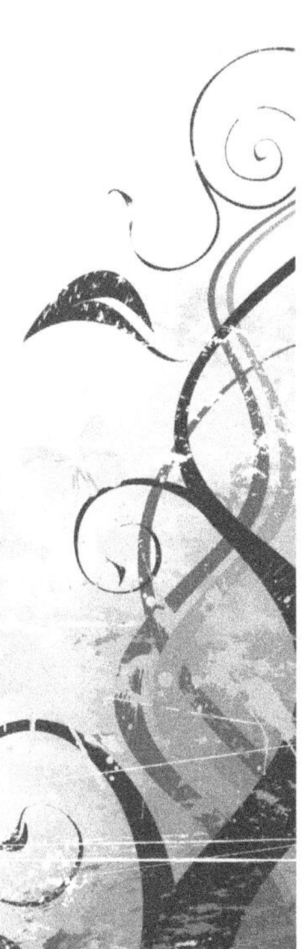

August 29

YOU CAN'T DO ANYTHING ABOUT
THE LENGTH OF YOUR LIFE,
BUT YOU CAN DO SOMETHING ABOUT
ITS WIDTH AND DEPTH.

—SHIRA TEHRANI

Year 1

Year 2

Year 3

Year 4

Year 5

I thank fate for
having made me born poor.
Poverty taught me the true value
of the gifts useful to life.

—Anatole France

August 30

Year 1

Year 2

Year 3

Year 4

Year 5

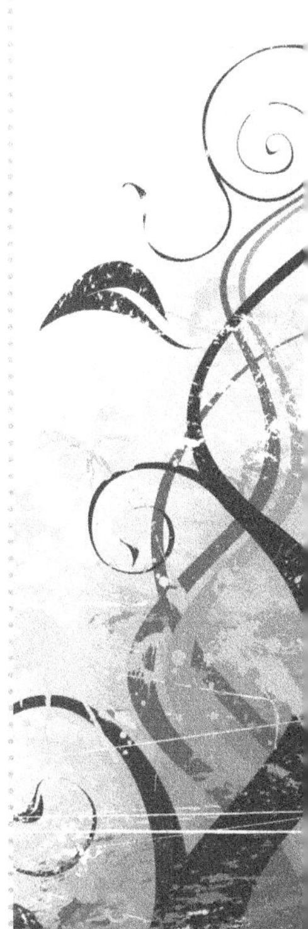

August 31

IN TIMES OF DOUBT AND INDECISION, CULTIVATE GRATITUDE.

—WALLACE D. WATTLES

Year 1

Year 2

Year 3

Year 4

Year 5

GRATITUDE IS BORN IN HEARTS THAT TAKE TIME TO COUNT UP PAST MERCIES.

—CHARLES E. JEFFERSON

Year 1

Year 2

Year 3

Year 4

Year 5

September 1

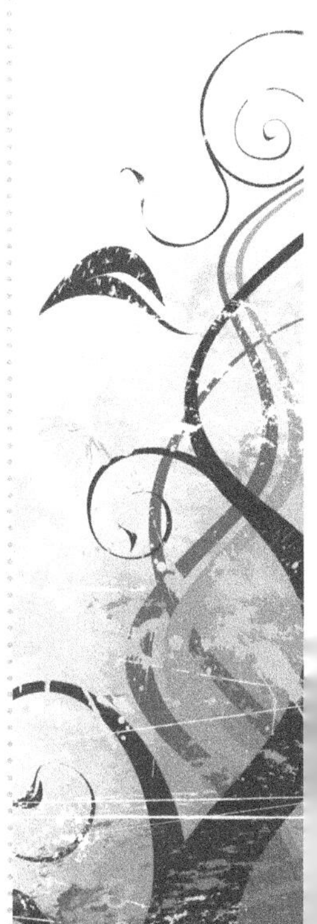

September 2

Every person has the power to make others happy. Some do it simply by entering a room—others by leaving the room. Some individuals leave trails of gloom; others, trails of joy. Some leave trails of hate and bitterness; others, trails of love

Year 1

Year 2

Year 3

Year 4

Year 5

AND HARMONY. SOME LEAVE TRAILS OF CYNICISM AND PESSIMISM; OTHERS TRAILS OF FAITH AND OPTIMISM. SOME LEAVE TRAILS OF CRITICISM AND RESIGNATION; OTHERS TRAILS OF GRATITUDE AND HOPE. WHAT KIND OF TRAILS DO YOU LEAVE?

—WILLIAM A. WARD

September 3

Year 1

Year 2

Year 3

Year 4

Year 5

September 4

THERE IS AS MUCH GREATNESS OF MIND IN ACKNOWLEDGING A GOOD TURN, AS IN DOING IT.

—SENECA

Year 1

Year 2

Year 3

Year 4

Year 5

September 5

WHAT WE DO FOR OURSELVES DIES WITH US. WHAT WE DO FOR OTHERS AND THE WORLD REMAINS AND IS IMMORTAL.

—ALBERT PIKE

Year 1

Year 2

Year 3

Year 4

Year 5

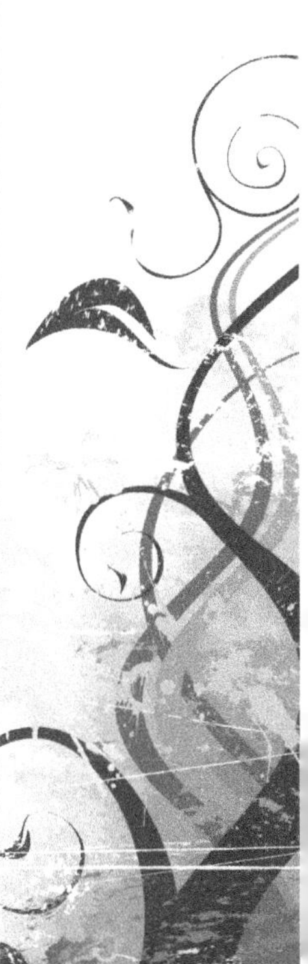

September 6

THE UNTHANKFUL HEART... DISCOVERS NO MERCIES; BUT LET THE THANKFUL HEART SWEEP THROUGH THE DAY AND, AS THE MAGNET FINDS THE IRON, SO IT WILL FIND, IN EVERY HOUR, SOME HEAVENLY BLESSINGS!

—Henry Ward Beecher

Year 1

Year 2

Year 3

Year 4

Year 5

Gratitude changes the pangs of memory into a tranquil joy.

—Dietrich Bonhoeffer

September 7

Year 1

Year 2

Year 3

Year 4

Year 5

September 8

So often we dwell on the things that seem impossible rather than on the things that are possible. So often we are depressed by what remains to be done and forget to be thankful for all that has been done.

—Marian Wright Edelman

Year 1

Year 2

Year 3

Year 4

Year 5

September 9

IF YOU WANT TO TURN YOUR LIFE AROUND, TRY THANKFULNESS. IT WILL CHANGE YOUR LIFE MIGHTILY.

—GERALD GOOD

Year 1

Year 2

Year 3

Year 4

Year 5

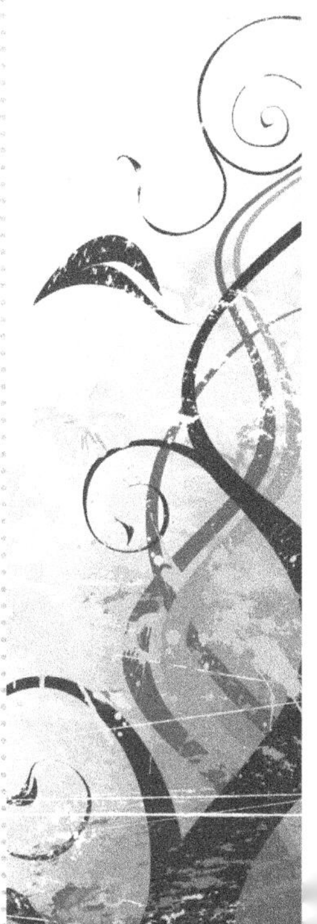

September 10

NO ONE IS AS CAPABLE OF GRATITUDE AS ONE WHO HAS EMERGED FROM THE KINGDOM OF NIGHT.

—ELIE WIESEL, HOLOCAUST SURVIVOR

Year 1

Year 2

Year 3

Year 4

Year 5

September 11

FIND THE GOOD—
AND PRAISE IT.

—ALEX HAILEY

Year 1

Year 2

Year 3

Year 4

Year 5

September 12

MOST HUMAN BEINGS HAVE AN ALMOST INFINITE CAPACITY FOR TAKING THINGS FOR GRANTED.

—ALDOUS HUXLEY

Year 1

Year 2

Year 3

Year 4

Year 5

September 13

WHEN I STARTED COUNTING
MY BLESSINGS,
MY WHOLE LIFE TURNED AROUND.

—WILLIE NELSON

Year 1

Year 2

Year 3

Year 4

Year 5

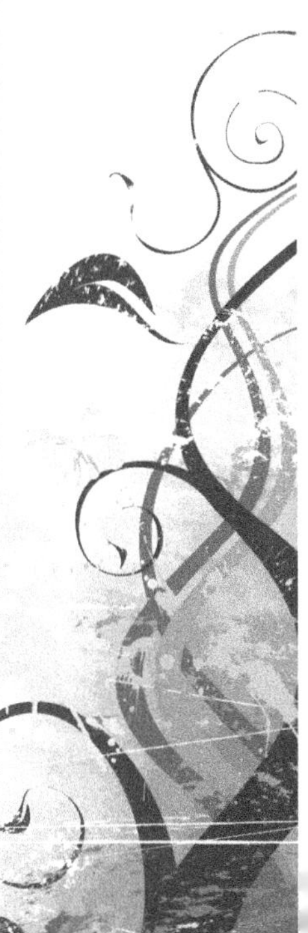

September 14

THE ENLIGHTENED GIVE THANKS FOR WHAT MOST PEOPLE TAKE FOR GRANTED. AS YOU BEGIN TO BE GRATEFUL FOR WHAT MOST PEOPLE TAKE FOR GRANTED, THAT VIBRATION OF GRATITUDE MAKES YOU MORE RECEPTIVE TO GOOD IN YOUR LIFE.

—Rev. Michael Beckwith

Year 1

Year 2

Year 3

Year 4

Year 5

September 15

A single grateful thought toward heaven is the most complete prayer.

—Gotthold Lessing

Year 1

Year 2

Year 3

Year 4

Year 5

September 16

FAITH IS BORN OF GRATITUDE.
THE GRATEFUL MIND CONTINUALLY
EXPECTS GOOD THINGS,
AND EXPECTATIONS BECOME FAITH.

—WALLACE WATTLES

Year 1

Year 2

Year 3

Year 4

Year 5

September 17

NOTHING PURCHASED CAN COME CLOSE TO THE RENEWED SENSE OF GRATITUDE FOR HAVING FAMILY AND FRIENDS.

—COURTLAND MILLOY

Year 1

Year 2

Year 3

Year 4

Year 5

September 18

GRATITUDE IS NOT ONLY
THE MEMORY BUT THE HOMAGE
OF THE HEART RENDERED
TO GOD FOR HIS GOODNESS.

—NATHANIEL P. WILLIS

Year 1

Year 2

Year 3

Year 4

Year 5

Thank God—every morning when you get up—that you have something to do which must be done, whether you like it or not. Being forced to work, and forced to do your best, will breed in you a hundred virtues which the idle never know.

—Charles Kingsley

September 19

Year 1

Year 2

Year 3

Year 4

Year 5

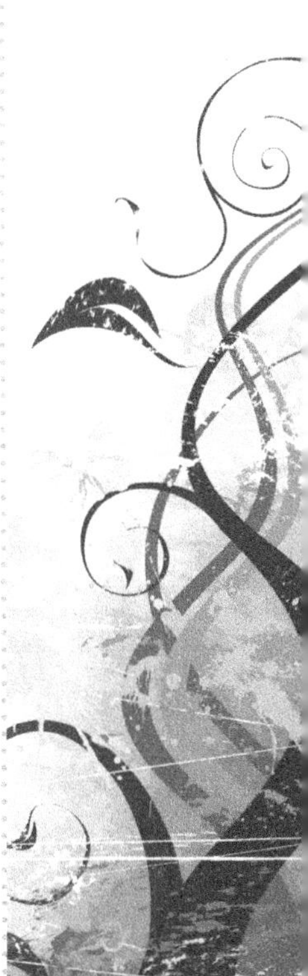

September 20

A man can only do
what a man can do.
But if he does that each day
he can sleep at night
and do it again the next day.

—Albert Schweitzer

Year 1

Year 2

Year 3

Year 4

Year 5

September 21

THOU WHO HAST GIVEN
SO MUCH TO ME,
GIVE ME ONE MORE THING...
A GRATEFUL HEART!

—GEORGE HERBERT

Year 1

Year 2

Year 3

Year 4

Year 5

September 22

Live your life so that the fear of death can never enter your heart. When you arise in the morning, give thanks for the morning light. Give thanks for your life and strength.

Year 1

Year 2

Year 3

Year 4

Year 5

September 23

GIVE THANKS FOR YOUR
FOOD AND FOR THE JOY OF LIVING.
AND IF PERCHANCE YOU SEE NO REASON
FOR GIVING THANKS, REST ASSURED
THE FAULT IS IN YOURSELF.

—CHIEF TECUMSEH, SHAWNEE INDIAN CHIEF

Year 1

Year 2

Year 3

Year 4

Year 5

September 24

When eating a fruit,
think of the person
who planted the tree.

—Vietnamese saying

Year 1

Year 2

Year 3

Year 4

Year 5

September 25

WHEN ASKED IF MY CUP
IS HALF-FULL OR HALF-EMPTY
MY ONLY RESPONSE IS THAT
I AM THANKFUL I HAVE A CUP.

—SAM LEFKOWITZ

Year 1

Year 2

Year 3

Year 4

Year 5

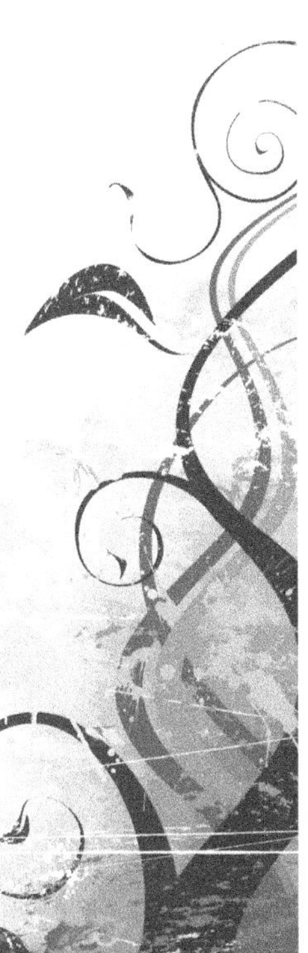

September 26

THE ONLY DISABILITY IN LIFE
IS A BAD ATTITUDE.

—Scott Hamilton

Year 1

Year 2

Year 3

Year 4

Year 5

September 27

EVERYTHING IS GIVEN TO ME AND I PASS IT ON. YOU MUST GIVE IF YOU WANT TO RECEIVE. LET THE CENTER OF YOUR BEING BE ONE OF GIVING, GIVING, GIVING. YOU CAN'T GIVE TOO MUCH, AND YOU WILL DISCOVER YOU CANNOT GIVE WITHOUT RECEIVING.

—PEACE PILGRIM

Year 1

Year 2

Year 3

Year 4

Year 5

WHAT HUMBUGS WE ARE,
WHO PRETEND TO LIVE FOR BEAUTY,
AND NEVER SEE THE DAWN!

—LOGAN PEARSALL SMITH

Year 1

Year 2

Year 3

Year 4

Year 5

September 29

IF YOU DON'T LIKE SOMETHING CHANGE IT. IF YOU CAN'T CHANGE IT, CHANGE YOUR ATTITUDE. DON'T COMPLAIN.

—MAYA ANGELOU

Year 1

Year 2

Year 3

Year 4

Year 5

September 30

GRATITUDE IS HEAVEN ITSELF.

—WILLIAM BLAKE

Year 1

Year 2

Year 3

Year 4

Year 5

October 1

Who does not thank for little will not thank for much.

—Estonian proverb

Year 1

Year 2

Year 3

Year 4

Year 5

October 2

A THANKFUL PERSON IS
THANKFUL UNDER ALL CIRCUMSTANCES.
A COMPLAINING SOUL COMPLAINS
EVEN IF HE LIVES IN PARADISE.

—BAHA'U'LLAH

Year 1

Year 2

Year 3

Year 4

Year 5

October 3

THE MOMENT ONE GIVES
CLOSE ATTENTION TO ANYTHING,
EVEN A BLADE OF GRASS,
IT BECOMES A MYSTERIOUS, AWESOME,
INDESCRIBABLY MAGNIFICENT
WORLD IN ITSELF.

—HENRY MILLER

Year 1

Year 2

Year 3

Year 4

Year 5

October 4

Keep your face to the sunshine
and you cannot see the shadows.

—Helen Keller

Year 1

Year 2

Year 3

Year 4

Year 5

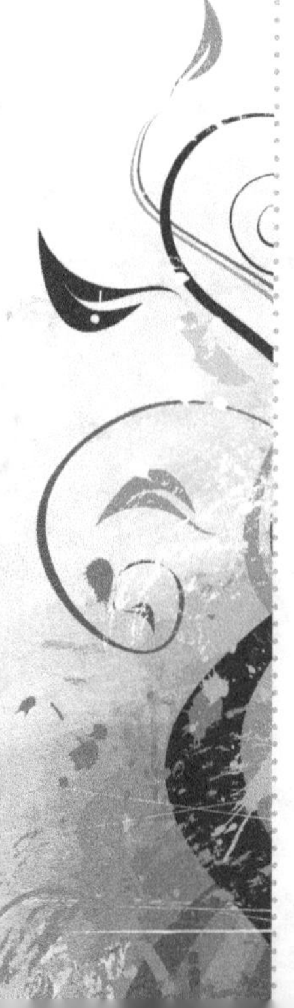

October 5

NOT WHAT WE HAVE
BUT WHAT WE ENJOY,
CONSTITUTES OUR ABUNDANCE.

—JOHN PETIT-SENN

Year 1

Year 2

Year 3

Year 4

Year 5

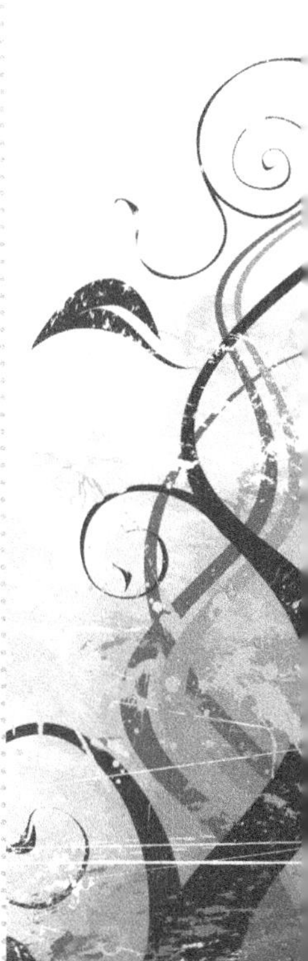

October 6

GRATITUDE IS ONE OF
THE SWEET SHORTCUTS TO FINDING
PEACE OF MIND AND HAPPINESS INSIDE.
NO MATTER WHAT'S GOING ON OUTSIDE
OF US, THERE'S ALWAYS SOMETHING
WE COULD BE GRATEFUL FOR.

—BARRY NEIL KAUFMAN

Year 1

Year 2

Year 3

Year 4

Year 5

October 7

WHAT WE SEE DEPENDS
MAINLY ON WHAT WE LOOK FOR.

—JOHN LUBBOCK

Year 1

Year 2

Year 3

Year 4

Year 5

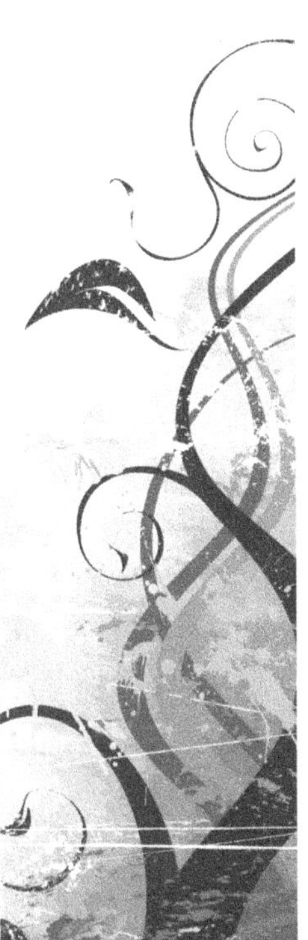

October 8

A BASIC LAW: THE MORE YOU PRACTICE THE ART OF THANKFULNESS, THE MORE YOU HAVE TO BE THANKFUL FOR. THIS, OF COURSE, IS A FACT. THANKFULNESS DOES TEND TO REPRODUCE IN KIND.

Year 1

Year 2

Year 3

Year 4

Year 5

THE ATTITUDE OF GRATITUDE REVITALIZES THE ENTIRE MENTAL PROCESS BY ACTIVATING ALL OTHER ATTITUDES, THUS STIMULATING CREATIVITY.

—NORMAN VINCENT PEALE

October 9

Year 1

Year 2

Year 3

Year 4

Year 5

October 10

If you don't feel grateful
for what you have,
what makes you think
you'll be happy with more?

—Unknown

Year 1

Year 2

Year 3

Year 4

Year 5

October 11

GRATITUDE IS LIKE A WARM BLANKET,
IT WARDS OFF THE ICY CHILL
OF DISCONTENT.

—C. BEAULIEU

Year 1

Year 2

Year 3

Year 4

Year 5

October 12

GENERALLY, APPRECIATION MEANS SOME BLEND OF THANKFULNESS, ADMIRATION, APPROVAL, AND GRATITUDE. IN THE FINANCIAL WORLD, SOMETHING THAT "APPRECIATES" GROWS IN VALUE. WITH THE POWER TOOL OF

Year 1

Year 2

Year 3

Year 4

Year 5

APPRECIATION, YOU GET THE BENEFIT OF BOTH PERSPECTIVES: AS YOU LEARN TO BE CONSISTENTLY THANKFUL AND APPROVING, YOUR LIFE WILL GROW IN VALUE.

—Doc Childre and Howard Martin, HeartMathSolution

October 13

Year 1

Year 2

Year 3

Year 4

Year 5

October 14

A MIND AND BODY
RESONATING WITH GRATITUDE
AND OTHER UPLIFTING FEELINGS
PROVIDES AN INHOSPITABLE
DWELLING PLACE FOR PAIN.

—ROBERT A. EMMONS, PH.D., THANKS!

Year 1

Year 2

Year 3

Year 4

Year 5

October 15

GRACE AND GRATITUDE
GO TOGETHER LIKE
HEAVEN AND EARTH.

—KARL BARTH

Year 1

Year 2

Year 3

Year 4

Year 5

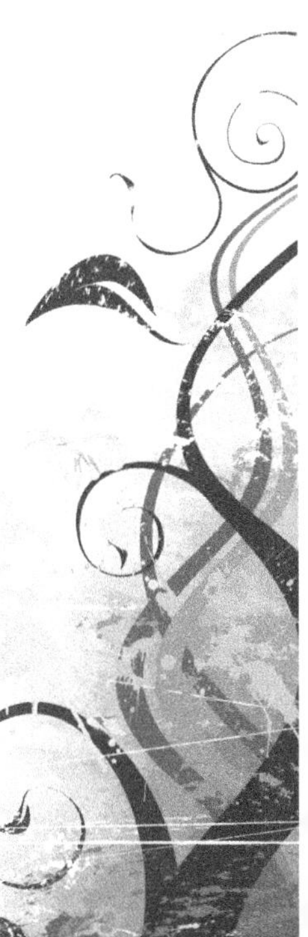

October 16

We who have lived in concentration camps can remember the men who walked through the huts comforting others, giving away their last piece of bread. They may have been few in numbers,

Year 1

Year 2

Year 3

Year 4

Year 5

BUT THEY OFFER SUFFICIENT PROOF THAT EVERYTHING CAN BE TAKEN FROM A MAN BUT ONE THING: THE LAST OF THE HUMAN FREEDOMS—TO CHOOSE ONE'S ATTITUDE IN ANY GIVEN SET OF CIRCUMSTANCES.

—Victor Frankl

October 17

Year 1

Year 2

Year 3

Year 4

Year 5

October 18

DO NOT SPOIL WHAT YOU HAVE
BY DESIRING WHAT YOU HAVE NOT;
BUT REMEMBER THAT WHAT YOU NOW
HAVE WAS ONCE AMONG
THE THINGS ONLY HOPED FOR.

—EPICURUS

Year 1

Year 2

Year 3

Year 4

Year 5

October 19

GRATITUDE IS THE REALIZATION THAT WE HAVE EVERYTHING WE NEED, AT THE MOMENT.

—ROBERT A. EMMONS, PH.D., THANKS!

Year 1

Year 2

Year 3

Year 4

Year 5

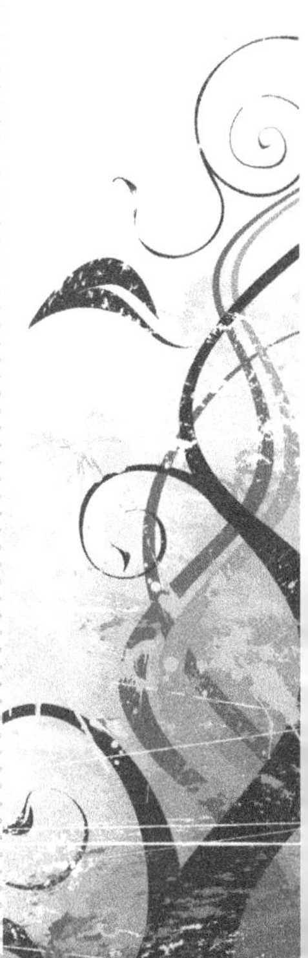

October 20

DIRECTING INGRATITUDE TOWARD OUR BENEFACTOR IS A WAY OF INFLICTING HARM UPON THAT PERSON.

—ROBERT A. EMMONS, PH.D., THANKS!

Year 1

Year 2

Year 3

Year 4

Year 5

October 21

Act with kindness,
but do not expect gratitude.

—Confucius

Year 1

Year 2

Year 3

Year 4

Year 5

October 22

TO IMPROVE IS TO CHANGE;
TO BE PERFECT IS TO CHANGE OFTEN.
—WINSTON CHURCHILL

Year 1

Year 2

Year 3

Year 4

Year 5

October 23

EACH DAY THAT I STAY AS A GUEST ON THIS GREEN EARTH SUDDENLY SEEMS LIKE OUTRAGEOUS GOOD FORTUNE.

—ONE WORLD TRADE CENTER SURVIVOR,
AS RELATED BY ROBERT A. EMMONS, PH.D. IN THANKS!

Year 1

Year 2

Year 3

Year 4

Year 5

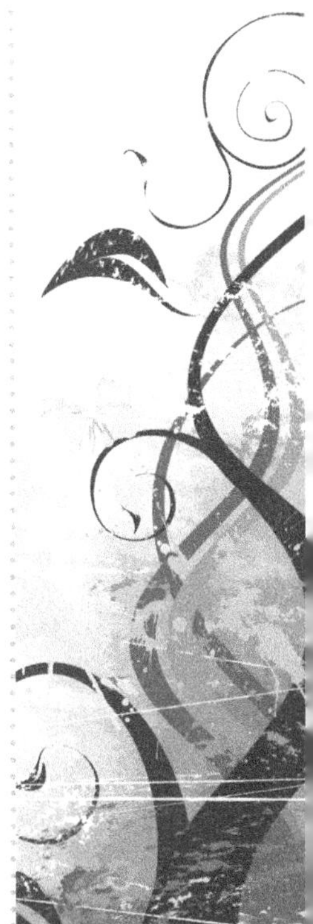

October 24

THIS SIMPLE PROCESS HAS THE POWER TO TRANSFORM YOUR LIFE. IF THE DUST SETTLES AND YOU'RE STILL STANDING, THERE'S A REASON FOR IT... NOW START WALKING! YOU CAN LEAVE THE KINGDOM OF NIGHT. YOU CAN START WALKING

Year 1

Year 2

Year 3

Year 4

Year 5

TOWARD THE GATES RIGHT NOW. YOUR FREEDOM BEGINS WITH BEING THANKFUL FOR THE SMALL THINGS—GAINING COURAGE AND STRENGTH TO REACH THE BIG THINGS.

—Elie Wiesel, Holocaust survivor

October 25

Year 1

Year 2

Year 3

Year 4

Year 5

October 26

GRATITUDE CAN TURN A MEAL INTO A FEAST, A HOUSE INTO A HOME, A STRANGER INTO A FRIEND.

—MELODY BEATTIE

Year 1

Year 2

Year 3

Year 4

Year 5

WE ARE WHAT WE THINK ABOUT ALL DAY LONG.

—RALPH WALDO EMERSON

October 27

Year 1

Year 2

Year 3

Year 4

Year 5

October 28

HAPPINESS LIES FOR THOSE WHO CRY,
THOSE WHO HURT, THOSE WHO
HAVE SEARCHED, AND THOSE WHO
HAVE TRIED FOR ONLY THEY CAN
APPRECIATE THE IMPORTANCE OF PEOPLE
WHO HAVE TOUCHED THEIR LIVES.

—Author Unknown

Year 1

Year 2

Year 3

Year 4

Year 5

I don't try to imagine a God;
it suffices to stand in awe
of the structure of the world,
insofar as it allows our inadequate
senses to appreciate it.

—Albert Einstein

October 29

Year 1

Year 2

Year 3

Year 4

Year 5

October 30

IN ORDER TO PLAN YOUR FUTURE WISELY, IT IS NECESSARY THAT YOU UNDERSTAND AND APPRECIATE YOUR PAST.

—JO COUDERT

Year 1

Year 2

Year 3

Year 4

Year 5

October 31

WE CAN ONLY APPRECIATE THE MIRACLE OF A SUNRISE IF WE HAVE WAITED IN THE DARKNESS. I WOULD RATHER BE ABLE TO APPRECIATE THINGS I CANNOT HAVE THAN TO HAVE THINGS I AM NOT ABLE TO APPRECIATE.

—ELBERT HUBBARD

Year 1

Year 2

Year 3

Year 4

Year 5

November 1

I have always thought it would be a blessing if each person could be blind and deaf for a few days during his early adult life. Darkness would make him appreciate sight; silence would teach him the joys of sound.

—Helen Keller

Year 1

Year 2

Year 3

Year 4

Year 5

November 2

LIFE IS FULL OF BEAUTY. NOTICE IT. NOTICE THE BUMBLE BEE, THE SMALL CHILD, AND THE SMILING FACES. SMELL THE RAIN, AND FEEL THE WIND. LIVE YOUR LIFE TO THE FULLEST POTENTIAL, AND FIGHT FOR YOUR DREAMS.

—ASHLEY SMITH

Year 1

Year 2

Year 3

Year 4

Year 5

November 3

IF THE STARS SHOULD APPEAR
BUT ONE NIGHT EVERY THOUSAND YEARS
HOW MAN WOULD MARVEL AND STARE.

—RALPH WALDO EMERSON

Year 1

Year 2

Year 3

Year 4

Year 5

November 4

APPRECIATION IS THE HIGHEST FORM OF PRAYER, FOR IT ACKNOWLEDGES THE PRESENCE OF GOOD WHEREVER YOU SHINE THE LIGHT OF YOUR THANKFUL THOUGHTS.

—Alan Cohen

Year 1

Year 2

Year 3

Year 4

Year 5

November 5

He enjoys much who is thankful for little.

—Thomas Secker

Year 1

Year 2

Year 3

Year 4

Year 5

Keep your eyes open to your mercies. The man who forgets to be thankful has fallen asleep in life.

—Robert Louis Stevenson

Year 1

Year 2

Year 3

Year 4

Year 5

November 7

We can be thankful to a friend for a few acres, or a little money; and yet for the freedom and command of the whole earth, and for the great benefits of our being, our life, health, and reason, we look upon ourselves as under no obligation.

—Lucius Annaeus Seneca

Year 1

Year 2

Year 3

Year 4

Year 5

November 8

ALL OUR DISCONTENTS ABOUT WHAT WE WANT APPEARED TO SPRING FROM THE WANT OF THANKFULNESS FOR WHAT WE HAVE.

—DANIEL DEFOE

Year 1

Year 2

Year 3

Year 4

Year 5

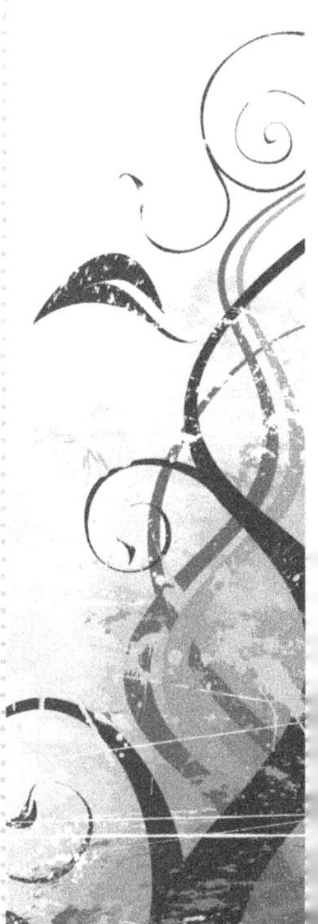

November 9

HEM YOUR BLESSINGS
WITH THANKFULNESS
SO THEY DON'T UNRAVEL.

—AUTHOR UNKNOWN

Year 1

Year 2

Year 3

Year 4

Year 5

November 10

It is impossible to feel grateful and depressed in the same moment.

—Naomi Williams

Year 1

Year 2

Year 3

Year 4

Year 5

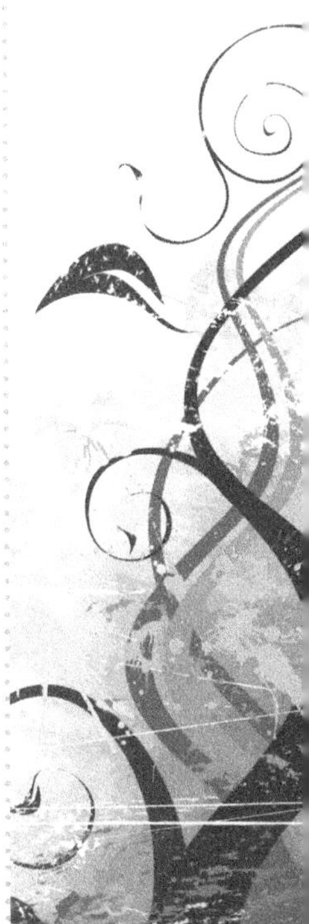

November 11

IT ISN'T WHAT YOU HAVE
IN YOUR POCKET
THAT MAKES YOU THANKFUL,
BUT WHAT YOU HAVE IN YOUR HEART.

—AUTHOR UNKNOWN

Year 1

Year 2

Year 3

Year 4

Year 5

November 12

As one person
I cannot change the world,
but I can change
the world of one person.

—Paul Shane Spear

Year 1

Year 2

Year 3

Year 4

Year 5

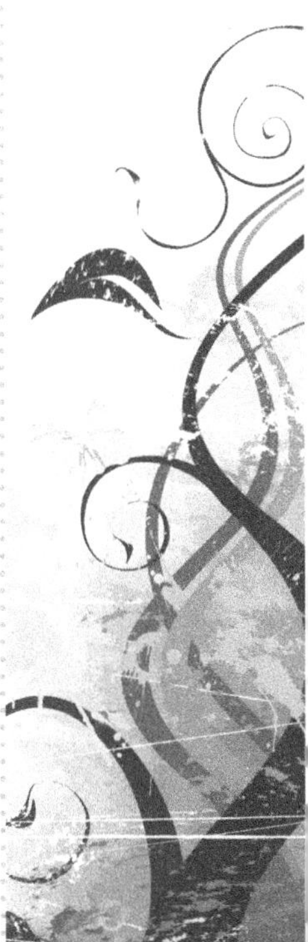

November 13

Just a "thank you"
is a mighty powerful prayer.
Says it all.

—Rosie Cash

Year 1

Year 2

Year 3

Year 4

Year 5

None is more impoverished than the one who has no gratitude. Gratitude is a currency that we can mint for ourselves, and spend without fear of bankruptcy.

—Fred De Witt Van Amburgh

November 14

Year 1

Year 2

Year 3

Year 4

Year 5

November 15

THERE ARE NO MISTAKES,
NO COINCIDENCES.
ALL EVENTS ARE BLESSINGS
GIVEN TO US TO LEARN FROM.

—ELISABETH KUBLER-ROSS

Year 1

Year 2

Year 3

Year 4

Year 5

PEOPLE WHO LIVE THE MOST FULFILLING LIVES ARE THE ONES WHO ARE ALWAYS REJOICING AT WHAT THEY HAVE.

—RICHARD CARLSON

November 16

Year 1

Year 2

Year 3

Year 4

Year 5

November 17

THE GRATEFUL MIND IS CONSTANTLY FIXED UPON THE BEST. THEREFORE IT TENDS TO BECOME THE BEST. IT TAKES THE FORM OR CHARACTER OF THE BEST, AND WILL RECEIVE THE BEST.

—WALLACE D. WATTLES

Year 1

Year 2

Year 3

Year 4

Year 5

November 18

THERE IS ALWAYS, ALWAYS, ALWAYS SOMETHING TO BE THANKFUL FOR.

—AUTHOR UNKNOWN

Year 1

Year 2

Year 3

Year 4

Year 5

November 19

THINGS TURN OUT BEST
FOR PEOPLE WHO MAKE THE BEST
OF THE WAY THINGS TURN OUT.

—JOHN WOODEN

Year 1

Year 2

Year 3

Year 4

Year 5

WHEREVER THERE IS A HUMAN BEING,
THERE IS AN OPPORTUNITY
FOR A KINDNESS.

—SENECA

Year 1

Year 2

Year 3

Year 4

Year 5

November 20

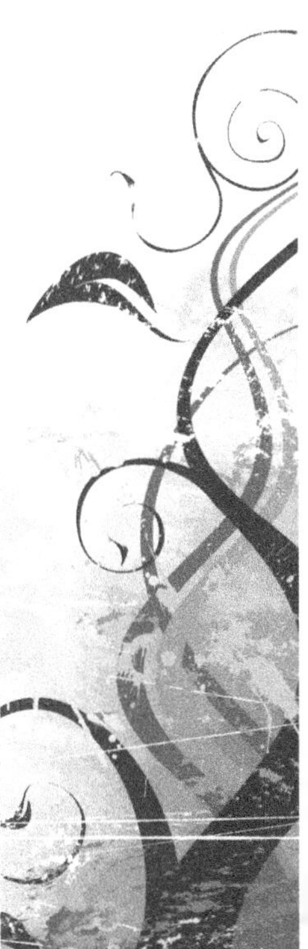

November 21

To live a life of gratitude is to open our eyes to the countless ways in which we are supported by the world around us. Such a life provides less space for our suffering because our attention

Year 1

Year 2

Year 3

Year 4

Year 5

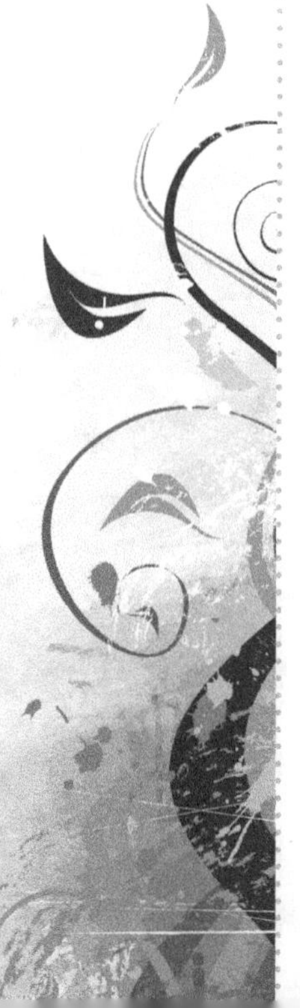

IS MORE BALANCED. WE ARE MORE OFTEN OCCUPIED WITH NOTICING WHAT WE ARE GIVEN, THANKING THOSE WHO HAVE HELPED US, AND REPAYING THE WORLD IN SOME CONCRETE WAY FOR WHAT WE ARE RECEIVING.

—GREGG KRECH

November 22

Year 1

Year 2

Year 3

Year 4

Year 5

November 23

YOU WON'T BE HAPPY WITH MORE
UNTIL YOU'RE HAPPY
WITH WHAT YOU'VE GOT.

—VIKI KING

Year 1

Year 2

Year 3

Year 4

Year 5

November 24

I FIND THAT THE MORE WILLING I AM TO BE GRATEFUL FOR THE SMALL THINGS IN LIFE, THE BIGGER STUFF JUST SEEMS TO SHOW UP FROM UNEXPECTED SOURCES, AND I AM CONSTANTLY LOOKING FORWARD TO EACH DAY WITH ALL THE SURPRISES THAT KEEP COMING MY WAY!

—LOUISE L. HAY

Year 1

Year 2

Year 3

Year 4

Year 5

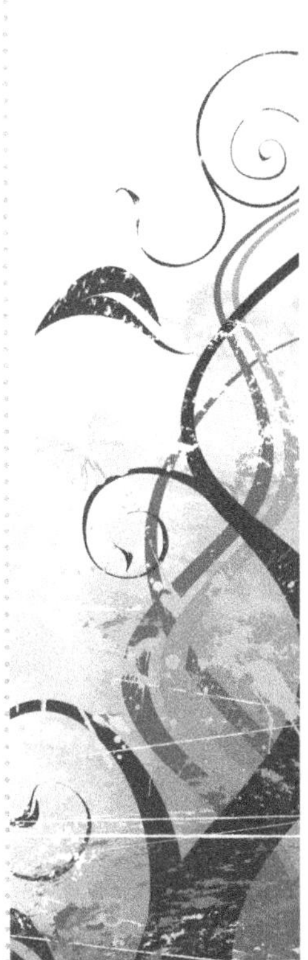

November 25

THE SIX MOST IMPORTANT WORDS:
I ADMIT I MADE A MISTAKE.
THE FIVE MOST IMPORTANT WORDS:
YOU DID A GOOD JOB.
THE FOUR MOST IMPORTANT WORDS:
WHAT IS **YOUR** OPINION?

Year 1

Year 2

Year 3

Year 4

Year 5

The three most important words:
If You Please.
The two most important words:
Thank You.
The one most important word: We.
The least important word: I.

—Author Unknown

November 26

Year 1

Year 2

Year 3

Year 4

Year 5

November 27

SAYING "THANK YOU" CREATES LOVE.

—DAPHNE ROSE KINGMA

Year 1

Year 2

Year 3

Year 4

Year 5

November 28

ONE CAN PAY BACK THE LOAN OF GOLD,
BUT ONE DIES FOREVER
IN DEBT TO THOSE WHO ARE KIND.

—AUTHOR UNKNOWN

Year 1

Year 2

Year 3

Year 4

Year 5

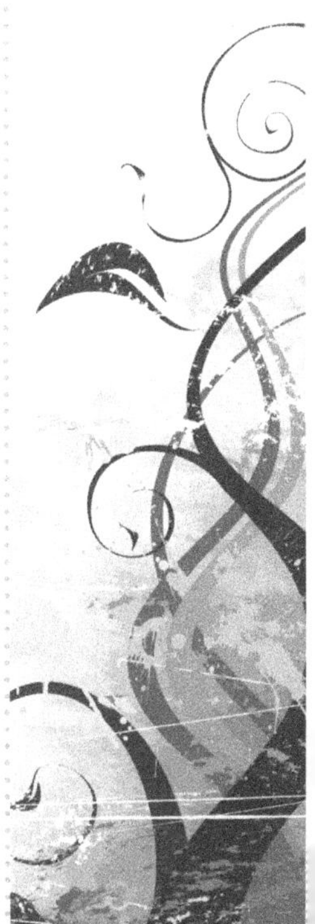

November 29

Try to do unto others
as you would have them do to you,
and do not be discouraged
if they fail sometimes. It is
much better that they should fail
than you should.

—Charles Dickens

Year 1

Year 2

Year 3

Year 4

Year 5

November 30

Be the change you want to see in the world.

—Ghandi

Year 1

Year 2

Year 3

Year 4

Year 5

December 1

THE ONLY PEOPLE WITH WHOM
YOU SHOULD TRY TO GET EVEN
ARE THOSE WHO HAVE HELPED YOU.

—JOHN E. SOUTHARD

Year 1

Year 2

Year 3

Year 4

Year 5

December 2

GRATITUDE IS A VACCINE,
AN ANTITOXIN,
AND AN ANTISEPTIC.

—JOHN HENRY JOWETT

Year 1

Year 2

Year 3

Year 4

Year 5

December 3

ONE KIND WORD CAN WARM
THREE WINTER MONTHS.

—Japanese Proverb

Year 1

Year 2

Year 3

Year 4

Year 5

December 4

NOT WHAT WE SAY
ABOUT OUR BLESSINGS,
BUT HOW WE USE THEM,
IS THE TRUE MEASURE OF
OUR THANKSGIVING.

—W.T. PURKISER

Year 1

Year 2

Year 3

Year 4

Year 5

December 5

WHAT WE ARE
IS GOD'S GIFT TO US.
WHAT WE BECOME IS
OUR GIFT TO GOD.

—ELEANOR POWELL

Year 1

Year 2

Year 3

Year 4

Year 5

December 6

Grace is available for each of us every day—our spiritual daily bread—but we've got to remember to ask for it with a grateful heart and not worry about whether there will be enough for tomorrow.

—Sarah Ban Breathnach

Year 1

Year 2

Year 3

Year 4

Year 5

December 7

REMEMBER THAT NOT TO BE HAPPY
IS NOT TO BE GRATEFUL.

—ELIZABETH CARTER

Year 1

Year 2

Year 3

Year 4

Year 5

December 8

MANY TIMES A DAY I REALIZE HOW MUCH MY OWN LIFE IS BUILT ON THE LABORS OF MY FELLOWMEN, AND HOW EARNESTLY I MUST EXERT MYSELF IN ORDER TO GIVE IN RETURN AS MUCH AS I HAVE RECEIVED.

—ALBERT EINSTEIN

Year 1

Year 2

Year 3

Year 4

Year 5

December 9

BLESSED BE THE LORD,
WHO DAILY LOADS US WITH BENEFITS...

—PSALM 68:19

Year 1

Year 2

Year 3

Year 4

Year 5

IT FEELS GOOD WHEN OUR EFFORTS ARE GRATEFULLY ACKNOWLEDGED AND HURTFUL WHEN OUR EFFORTS ARE MET WITH INDIFFERENCE, GRUDGINGLY OFFERED THANKS, OR INGRATITUDE.

—Robert A. Emmons, Ph.D., thanks!

Year 1

Year 2

Year 3

Year 4

Year 5

December 10

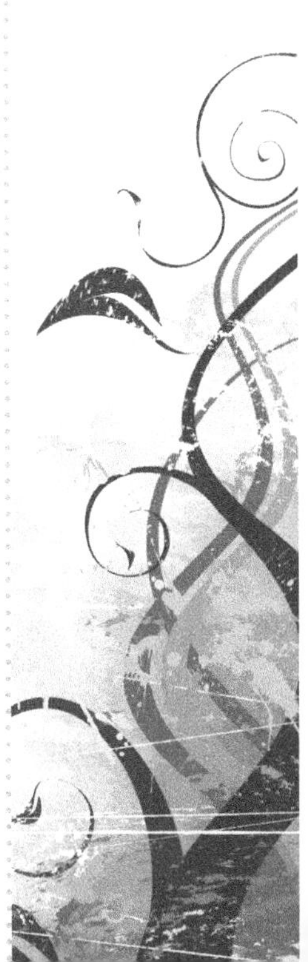

December 11

WE ARE ALL MOTIVATED
BY A KEEN DESIRE FOR PRAISE,
AND THE BETTER A MAN IS,
THE MORE HE IS INSPIRED TO GLORY.

—CICERO

Year 1

Year 2

Year 3

Year 4

Year 5

WE HAVE TO ACCEPT
THE CONSEQUENCES OF EVERY DEED,
WORD, AND THOUGHT
THROUGHOUT OUR LIFETIME.

—ELISABETH KUBLER-ROSS

Year 1

Year 2

Year 3

Year 4

Year 5

December 12

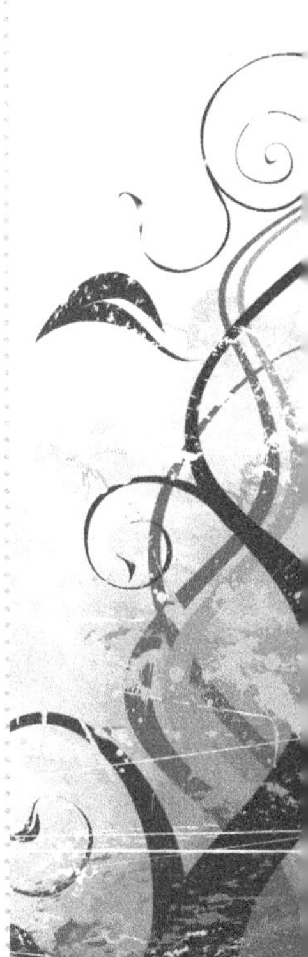

December 13

TRY NOT TO BECOME
A MAN OF SUCCESS
BUT A MAN OF VALUE.

—ALBERT EINSTEIN

Year 1

Year 2

Year 3

Year 4

Year 5

December 14

EVERY PROBLEM HAS A GIFT FOR YOU IN ITS HANDS.

—RICHARD BACH

Year 1

Year 2

Year 3

Year 4

Year 5

December 15

IF THERE IS ANY KINDNESS
I CAN SHOW, OR ANY GOOD THING
I CAN DO TO ANY FELLOW BEING,
LET ME DO IT NOW, AND NOT DETER
OR NEGLECT IT, AS I SHALL
NOT PASS THIS WAY AGAIN.

—WILLIAM PENN

Year 1

Year 2

Year 3

Year 4

Year 5

LET NEVER DAY NOR NIGHT
UNHALLOWED PASS,
BUT STILL REMEMBER
WHAT THE LORD HATH DONE.

—WILLIAM SHAKESPEARE

December 16

Year 1

Year 2

Year 3

Year 4

Year 5

December 17

DEPRIVED THINKING
TURNS GOOD THINGS INTO LESS,
OR WORSE, INTO NOTHING.
GRATEFUL THINKING TURNS
THINGS INTO MORE.

—MELODY BEATTIE

Year 1

Year 2

Year 3

Year 4

Year 5

December 18

FOR ME, GIVING THANKS IS A SIGN OF APPRECIATION AND GRATITUDE THAT ALSO BRINGS ABOUT A DEEP SENSE OF PEACE.

—WALLY AMOS

Year 1

Year 2

Year 3

Year 4

Year 5

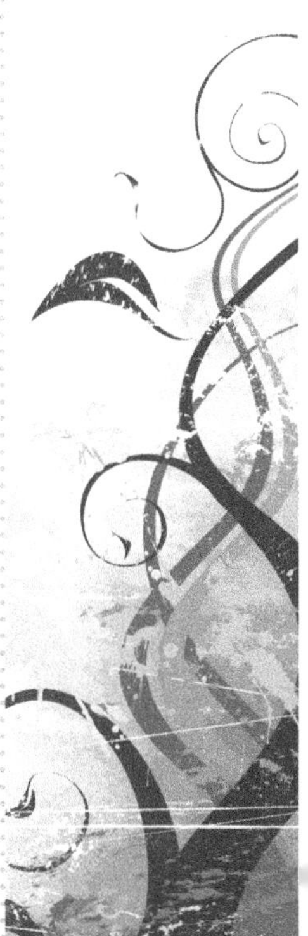

December 19

PROSPERITY DEPENDS MORE
ON WANTING WHAT YOU HAVE
THAN HAVING WHAT YOU WANT.

—GEOFFREY F. ABERT

Year 1

Year 2

Year 3

Year 4

Year 5

December 20

It is never too late
to be what we
might have been.

—George Eliot

Year 1

Year 2

Year 3

Year 4

Year 5

December 21

ONCE WE DISCOVER
HOW TO APPRECIATE THE
TIMELESS VALUES IN OUR DAILY
EXPERIENCES, WE CAN ENJOY
THE BEST THINGS IN LIFE.

—HARRY HEPNER

Year 1

Year 2

Year 3

Year 4

Year 5

December 22

Is there some principal of nature which states that we never know the quality of what we have until it is gone?

—Elbert Hofstadter

Year 1

Year 2

Year 3

Year 4

Year 5

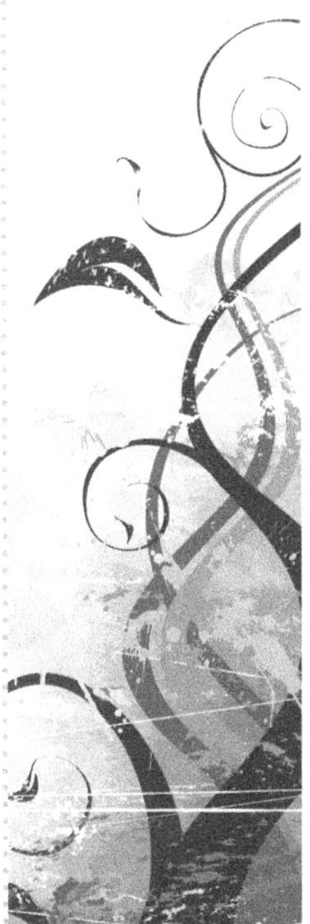

December 23

LIFE IS CHANGE. GROWTH IS OPTIONAL.
CHOOSE WISELY.

—KAREN KAISER CLARK

Year 1

Year 2

Year 3

Year 4

Year 5

December 24

BETTER TO LOSE COUNT
WHILE NAMING YOUR BLESSINGS
THAN TO LOSE YOUR BLESSINGS TO
COUNTING YOUR TROUBLES.

—MALTBIE D. BABCOCK

Year 1

Year 2

Year 3

Year 4

Year 5

December 25

If the sight of the blue skies fills you with joy, if a blade of grass springing up in the fields has power to move you, if the simple things of nature have a message that you understand, rejoice, for your soul is alive.

—Eleonora Duse

Year 1

Year 2

Year 3

Year 4

Year 5

DON'T EVER SAVE ANYTHING
FOR A SPECIAL OCCASION.
BEING ALIVE IS
THE SPECIAL OCCASION.

—AUTHOR UNKNOWN

Year 1

Year 2

Year 3

Year 4

Year 5

December 26

December 27

THE RICHEST PERSON
IS THE ONE WHO IS CONTENTED
WITH WHAT HE HAS.

—Robert C. Savage

Year 1

Year 2

Year 3

Year 4

Year 5

I don't think of all the misery but of the beauty that still remains.

—Anne Frank

Year 1

Year 2

Year 3

Year 4

Year 5

December 28

December 29

MAY YOU ALWAYS WALK IN BEAUTY.

—ANCIENT PRAYER

Year 1

Year 2

Year 3

Year 4

Year 5

One of the sanest, surest, and most generous joys of life comes from being happy over the good fortune of others.

—Archibald Rutledge

Year 1

Year 2

Year 3

Year 4

Year 5

December 30

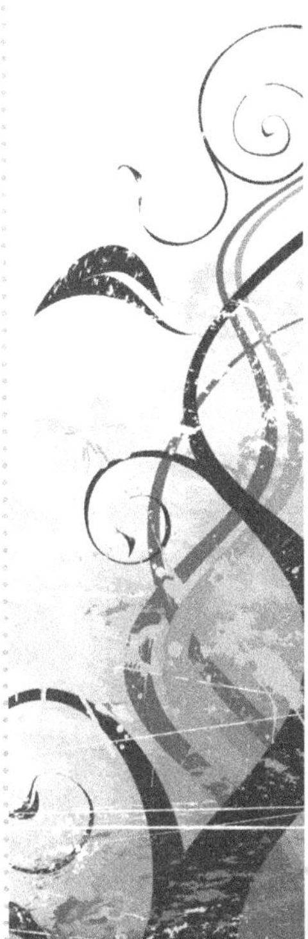

December 31

What sunshine is to flowers,
smiles are to humanity.
These are but trifles, to be sure;
but, scattered along life's pathway,
the good they do is inconceivable.

—Joseph Addison

Year 1

Year 2

Year 3

Year 4

Year 5

Gratitude Expressions was created as a companion to *Thank Everybody for Everything! Grow Your Life and Business with Gratitude*, by Deborah Roser and Peggy Hoyt. *Thank Everybody for Everything! Grow Your Life and Business with Gratitude* is available wherever *Gratitude Expressions* is sold, or you may contact the authors directly or visit ThankEverybodyForEverything.com.

About The Authors

Deborah E. Roser, J.D.

Debbie lived life to the fullest, enjoying a career as an attorney, author and entrepreneur. She believed we each have the power to create a positive shift in our lives – and those of others- by recognizing our blessings and sharing our gratitude. She co-authored this journal as well as *Thank Everybody for Everything – Grow Your Life and Business with Gratitude; Straight Talk! The Truth about Estate Planning and Straight Talk! What to Do When Someone Dies*. She also authored *One More Conversation*. All of her books are available on Amazon.com.

She was a dream-follower and adventurer. In 2007, she and husband Craig sold their home and left their work in Connecticut for a two-year sailing hiatus that took them up and down the Eastern Seaboard from Maine to Key West including some jaunts to Bermuda and the Bahamas. As cruisers, they were part of an amazing community of caring, loving and giving individuals and made lifetime friends. Debbie also partnered with friends, Radeen Cochran and Vanessa Williams, to launch an interactive website for women sailors to associate, learn from and help each other.

In March 2013, Debbie was diagnosed with Lou Gehrig's disease (ALS). She died on January 17, 2014.

Peggy R. Hoyt, J.D., M.B.A, B.C.S.*

(*board certified specialist in wills, trusts and estates and elder law)

Peggy is an attorney, author and entrepreneur who reflects her passion for pets in almost everything she does. She comes by her love of animals naturally as her father was the President and CEO of The Humane Society of the United States from 1970-1997.

Peggy and her law partner, Randy Bryan, own and operate The Law Offices of Hoyt & Bryan, LLC—Family Wealth & Legacy Counsellors, in Oviedo, Florida. Both Peggy and Randy are dual Florida Bar board certified in Wills, Trusts and Estates as well as Elder Law. Their firm limits its practice to estate planning and elder law issues including the creation, maintenance and administration of estate plans that "work." Areas of expertise also include planning for special needs family members, unmarried couples, business succession and of course, pets.

Peggy loves to write. Her first book, *All My Children Wear Fur Coats – How to Leave a Legacy for Your Pet,* (LegacyForYourPet. com) was inspired by her pets, currently three horses, five dogs and a constantly changing number of cats. Other co-authored books include *Special People, Special Planning- Creating a Safe Legal Haven for Families with Special Needs; Loving Without a License – An Estate Planning Survival Guide for Unmarried Couples and Same Sex Partners; A Matter of Trust – The Importance of Personal Instruction; Women in Transition – Navigating the Legal and Financial Challenges in Your Life; Like a Library Burning – Saving and Sharing Stories of a Lifetime; Thank Everybody for Everything – How to Grow Your Life and Business with Gratitude; Straight Talk – The Truth About Estate Planning; and Straight Talk – What To Do When Someone Dies.*

Peggy's interests are varied and include her role as Senior Manager in SendOutCards as a Card Diva. She uses the SendOutCards system both personally and professionally and has adopted a philosophy of "making a living through giving." She is also active in a variety of organizations, including WealthCounsel, past Chair of the General Practice, Solo and Small Firm Section of the Florida Bar and as a member of the Elder Law Section, Academy of Florida Elder Law Attorneys (AFELA) and the Central Florida Estate Planning Council. Peggy is a regular speaker on estate planning and elder law topics, as well as practice management including team training and marketing. Her latest ventures include *MyPetWill.com* and *PetFriendly.love*, both inspired by her love of pets.

Peggy is married to Joe Allen and spends her "free" time playing with her dogs and training for limited distance endurance and competitive trail riding events on her rescue Horse, Heaven.

To contact Peggy:
Peggy@HoytBryan.com
HoytBryan.com
PeggyHoyt.com
GratitudePartners.com
CardDivas.com